THE GREEK ISLANDS

Genius Loci

View of Naxos island seen through the monumental doorway of the Archaic temple.
Thomas Hope (1769-1831) Watercolour, 44 x 29 cm. Benaki Museum, Inv. No. 27375.
© 2010 Benaki Museum, Athens.

Author's acknowledgements

This series of twenty books covering the Aegean Islands is the fruit of many years of solitary dedication to a job difficult to accomplish given the extent of the subject matter and the geography involved. My belief throughout has been that only what is seen with the eyes can trustfully be written about; and to that end I have attempted to walk, ride, drive, climb, sail and swim these Islands in order to inspect everything talked about here. There will be errors in this text inevitably for which, although working in good faith, I alone am responsible. Notwithstanding, I am confident that these are the best, most clearly explanatory and most comprehensive artistic accounts currently available of this vibrant and historically dense corner of the Mediterranean.

Professor Robin Barber, author of the last, general, *Blue Guide to Greece* (based in turn on Stuart Rossiter's masterful text of the 1960s), has been very generous with support and help; and I am also particularly indebted to Charles Arnold for meticulously researched factual data on the Islands and for his support throughout this project. I could not have asked for a more saintly and helpful editor, corrector and indexer than Judy Tither. Efi Stathopoulou, Peter Cocconi, Marc René de Montalembert, Valentina Ivancich, William Forrester and Geoffrey Cox have all given invaluable help; and I owe a large debt of gratitude to John and Jay Rendall for serial hospitality and encouragement. For companionship on many journeys, I would like to thank a number of dear friends: Graziella Seferiades, Ivan Tabares, Matthew Kidd, Martin Leon, my group of Louisianan friends, and my brother Iain— all of whose different reactions to and passions for Greece have been a constant inspiration.

This work is dedicated with admiration and deep affection to Ivan de Jesus Tabares-Valencia who, though a native of the distant Andes mountains, from the start understood the profound spiritual appeal of the Aegean world.

McGILCHRIST'S GREEK ISLANDS

15. NORTHERN DODECANESE

KALYMNOS, TELENDOS, LEROS, PATMOS, LIPSI, ARKI
&
AGATHONISI

GENIUS LOCI PUBLICATIONS
London

McGilchrist's Greek Islands 15. Northern Dodecanese
First edition

Published by Genius Loci Publications
54 Eccleston Road, London W13 0RL

Nigel McGilchrist © 2010
Nigel McGilchrist has asserted his moral rights.

ISBN 978-1-907859-11-3

A CIP catalogue record of this book is available from the British Library.

The author and publisher cannot accept responsibility or liability for
information contained herein, this being in some cases difficult to verify
and subject to change.

Layout and copy-editing by Judy Tither

Cover design by Kate Buckle

Maps and plans by Nick Hill Design

Printed and bound in Great Britain by TJ International Ltd, Padstow,
Cornwall

The island maps in this series are based on the cartography of
Terrain Maps
Karneadou 4, 106 75 Athens, Greece
T: +30 210 609 5759, Fx: +30 210 609 5859
terrain@terrainmaps.gr
www.terrainmaps.gr

This book is one of twenty which comprise the complete, detailed
manuscript which the author prepared for the *Blue Guide: Greece,
the Aegean Islands* (2010), and on which the *Blue Guide* was
based. Some of this text therefore appears in the *Blue Guide*.

A NOTE ON THE TEXT & MAPS

Some items in the text are marked with an asterisk: these may be monuments, landscapes, curiosities or individual artefacts and works of art. The asterisk is not simply an indication of the renown of a particular place or item, but is intended to draw the reader's attention to things that have a uniquely interesting quality or are of particular beauty.

A small number of hotels and eateries are also marked with asterisks in the *Practical Information* sections, implying that their quality or their setting is notably special. These books do not set out to be guides to lodging and eating in the Islands, and our recommendations here are just an attempt to help with a few suggestions for places that have been selected with an eye to simplicity and unpretentiousness. We believe they may be the kind of places that a reader of this book would be seeking and would enjoy.

On the island maps:

∴   denotes a site with visible prehistoric or ancient remains

✝   denotes a church referred to in the text
(on Island Maps only rural churches are marked)

✚   denotes a monastery, convent or large church referred to in the text

⊞   denotes a Byzantine or Mediaeval castle

⛲   denotes an important fresh-water or geothermic spring

⛴   denotes a harbour with connecting ferry services

Road and path networks:

-    a continuous line denotes a metalled road or unsurfaced track feasible for motors

-    a dotted line denotes footpath only

CONTENTS

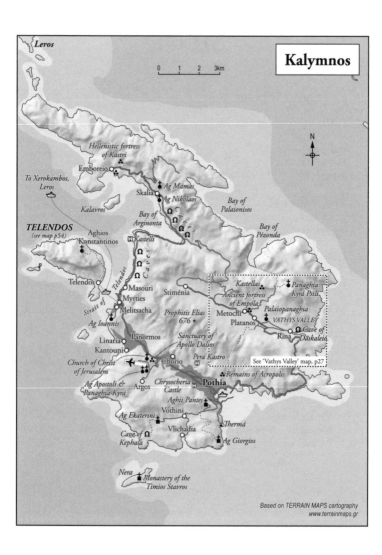

Leros

Kalymnos

0 1 2 3km

N

Hellenistic fortress of Kastri

Emboreio

To Xerokambos, Leros

♣ *Ag Mámas*

Skalia

Ag Nikólaos

Kalavros

Bay of Arginonta

Bay of Palaionisos

TELENDOS
(see map p54)

Aghios Konstantinos

☐ *Kastelli*

Bay of Pézonda

Telendos

Kastellas

Ancient fortress of Empolas

♣ *Panaghia Kyrá Psilí*

Masouri

Myrties

Stiménia

Metochí

Palaiopanaghia

VATHYS VALLEY

Melitsacha

Ag Ioannis

Platanos

Prophitis Elias 676 +

Riná *Cave of Daskaleió*

Linaria

Pánormos

Sanctuary of Apollo Dálios

Kantouni

Church of Christ of Jerusalem

Chorio

See 'Vathys Valley' map, p27

Pera Kastro

☐

Remains of Acropolis

Ag Apostoli & Panaghia Kyrá

Argos

Chrysocheriá Castle

Pothia

Aghii Pantes

Ag Ekaterini

Vothini

Vlichadia

Thermá

Cave of Kephalá

Ag Giorgios

Nera ■ *Monastery of the Timios Stavros*

Based on *TERRAIN MAPS* cartography
www.terrainmaps.gr

KALYMNOS

Kalymnos delights with its combination of easy normality and vivid geographical contrasts: a skeleton of rock-bare mountains breached by shallow plains of intense green fertility; waters, once renowned for the sponges in their limpid depths, reflecting mountain ridges and summits shot through with caves that are famous among pot-holers and rock-climbers; and, set in contrast to all this ruggedness, the island's capital, Pothia, which has a busy metropolitan feel. Large for the overall size of the island and built on the wealth that came from fishing and sponge-trading, Pothia is a pleasant and businesslike port with none of the artificiality which comes of picturesqueness or over-dependence on tourism.

The island's landscape is everywhere profoundly sculpted and folded. An earthquake in the 6th century is commonly supposed to have changed the shape of Kalymnos by separating Telendos (now an islet) from the main body of the island. In fact, this separation is more likely to have been the result of a much older geological activity which has fashioned the waters and mountains of the west of the island into one of the most beautiful and dramatic marine landscapes in the Aegean.

Even more than on Kos, there is an astonishing quantity of Early Christian remains—basilicas, settlements, bath-houses, tombs—on Kalymnos. It emphasises how confident and populous the Christian community was that established itself on the island in the early 500s, only to be devastated first by the earthquake of 554 and then cut short by hostile Arab incursions a hundred years later, which left the inhabitants by the end of the 7th century clinging to refuges in remote mountain fastnesses such as Aghios Konstantinos on Telendos. Although Telendos and Vathys are the densest areas of these palaeochristian remains, early churches can be found in all corners of the island and their greatest treasures are often their fine mosaic floors. Many were constructed over remains from pagan antiquity, such as the memorable structure of the church of Christ of Jerusalem, built from demolished blocks of the important Calydnian sanctuary of Apollo. Its elements constitute a veritable museum of ancient inscriptions. The island has two fortified sites of the Hellenistic period, which are both unusual in character—an extensive complex at Empola (Vathys), and another at the dramatic and hidden site of Kastri in the north of the island.

Kalymnos is an island with a strong sense of identity: a perceptible accent of its own in spoken Greek, and a proud perpetuation of Byzantine names and old-fashioned, more poetic, forms of address and salutation. A number of small museums on the island celebrate this cultural conservatism and diversity, as well as giving a valuable picture of the remarkable—and often tragic—story of the island's pre-eminence in the world's sponge-trade.

HISTORY

The name '*Kalymna*', often taken to refer to its several good ('*kali-*') harbours ('*-limin*'), only appears in the 4th century BC; until then, the island is referred to as '*Kalydna*' (beautiful waters) and, by Homer (*Iliad* II. 676/7), in the plural form, 'Calydnian islands', referring presumably to a group, including also Pserimos and possibly Leros. The island's many caves have yielded a quantity of material—burnished and decorated vases, tools and figurines—providing evidence of Late Neolithic (4th millennium BC) and Early Bronze Age settlement, with continued use through into Mycenaean times (especially in the cave of Daskaleió in the area of Vathýs). The first settlers in early historic times were from Epidaurus in the Argolid: the main centres of habitation, determined as always by the presence of fresh water, were in the same two valleys that are populated today. The island was organised into seven demes, and a silver coinage was issued in the 6th century BC: a warrior's helmeted head bearing the letter 'A' (for Antiphos, one of the island's Heroic founders) on the obverse, and a lyre (for the predominating cult of Apollo) on the reverse. The important and early sanctuary of Apollo was at *Damos*, on the low saddle near the modern town of Chorió. After the Battle of Salamis in 480 BC, where the Kalymniots fought for the Persian side (together with Kos) under the command of Queen Artemisia of Halicarnassus, the island turned to Athens and became a member of the Delian League. In the aftermath of the death of Alexander the Great, the southeast Aegean saw considerable turmoil in the subsequent struggles of succession: it is to this period that many of the fortifications on the island date. In 205/4 BC Kalymnos became linked and subject to Kos by an arrangement of '*homopoliteia*' (a constitutional joining of cities), and its history thereafter follows that of its larger neighbour. Together with Kos, it benefited from the same *immunitas* bestowed by the Emperor Claudius in 53 AD at the instigation of his personal physician, who was a native of Kos. Strabo noted the particularly good quality of the island's honey (*Geog.* X, 19)

A flourishing Early Christian community on Kalymnos, comparable, in proportion to its size, to that on Kos, has left behind the remains of a large number of once richly decorated Palaeochristian churches, but a catastrophic earthquake in 554 AD destroyed many of them. Subsequent Arab invasions in the 7th century led to progressive abandonment of the coastal settlements. After 1204 Venetian and Genoese overlords ruled the island until it came under the control of the Knights of St John of Rhodes in 1313. They held and fortified Kalymnos until their defeat in Rhodes by Suleiman the Magnificent in 1522/3.

After 1523, the island maintained a considerable degree of autonomy under the Ottoman occupation. This gave the opportunity—as it did similarly on Symi—for the fishing and sponge trades to bring prosperity and considerable urban development, especially in the 19th century. A new island capital at Póthia was created and laid out, and the island's population more than quadrupled between 1821 (5,000) and 1912 (23,000). The Italian occupation after 1912 brought considerable economic and cultural restrictions, however, and the historically independent spirit of the Kalymniots rebelled against the imposition of Italian language and the elimination of Greek in schools; resentment was further fuelled by interference with the Orthodox Church. Riots were suppressed in 1935, and many islanders were jailed or exiled by the Italians. During and immediately after the Second World War, the population was depleted by emigration to the Middle East and to the United States. The island joined the Greek State together with the other Dodecanese Islands in March 1948. Kalymnos is the only island in the Dodecanese still to have preserved a small sponge-fishing fleet.

The guide to the island has been divided into three sections:-
* *Póthia, the Vathýs Valley, and the south of the island*
* *Chorió and the north of the island*
* *The isle of Telendos*

POTHIA,
THE VATHYS VALLEY &
THE SOUTH OF THE ISLAND

POTHIA

The island's port, **Póthia**, which grew in the 19th century from a small fishing village into the island's capital, has a noticeable sense of compression as if the space between the stark limestone slopes to either side were not sufficient to contain its vibrant activity. Here—as in Ermoupolis on Syros—the productive everyday business of a large local population is first and foremost, and tourism is just a small and incidental addition to it. None of the introspective lassitude that has overcome Symi after the demise of its sponge-trade is to be found here; commercial activity has simply moved on and concentrated itself in different fields.

Viewed from an arriving boat, the city is dominated by the huge standing cross and modern convent of Aghii Pantes, often called 'Aghios Savvás' nowadays, high up on the southwestern mountain; on the slopes below it is the older, Ottoman and 19th century **commercial quarter** of

the town—a network of narrow streets bordered by balconied, stone buildings, with pedimented windows and
sternly rusticated corners. Across, at the opposite northeastern side of the bay, are the old **boat-yards** and chan-
dlers' shops of the area of **Lafássi**. Just inland of there,
and slightly to the west along the foot of the hills to the
north, is the main **residential area** of stately, 19th century
mansions—some with gardens—known as **Evangelís-
tria**. In between these two poles stretches the waterfront,
punctuated at its centre by the low domed mass of the
former '**Kalymnos Administration Building**', originally
built between 1926–28 by the Italian colonial masters,
and then significantly enlarged in 1934. The difference
between the two campaigns of building is instructive: the
early part, put up in the 1920s by Florestano di Fausto,
is the main block (west) standing further in from the
harbour front, designed in whimsical style with serifed
arches and decorated, ceramic panels; by contrast, Armando Bernabiti's addition of 1934 to the east, with its
more severe lines and squat cupolas, dates from a period
when the Italian regime had begun to flex its totalitarian
muscles. Contemporary with Bernabiti's addition and in
similar style is the **market building**, just to the north, designed by Rodolfo Petracco.

The rest of the waterfront is a heterogeneous assemblage of buildings of different periods, including a few well-preserved neoclassical façades with wrought-iron balconies. One interesting building towards the southern end of the front, is the former *Anagnostírion* (reading-room) '*Ai Musai*' built in 1904: above the Ionic pilasters of its entrance are three bronze panels depicting scenes of Kalymniot life by the local artist, Michalis Kokkinos (1900–90): the interior (which is now an unpretentious *kafeneion*) preserves many of the paintings and portrait busts of the original décor. Other works by Kokkinos can be seen at several points along the waterfront: (from west to east) a *Poseidon*; the *Sponge-diver*; a *Nike* on a plinth decorated with relief panels of *Scenes of sponge-fishing*. The bronze portrait statue of the academic and doctor, **Skevos Zervos** (1875–1966), who was an important political fighter for the emancipation of the Dodecanese, is the work of Kokkinos's daughter, Irini. This stands in front of the south side of the Kos Administration Building. On the north side of the building is a square, bounded to the north by the **church of the Metamorphosis** (1861): the great **iconostasis** (1877) in gilded grey marble from Tinos designed and carved by the Tiniot sculptor, Giannoulis Chalepás (1851–1938), dominates the interior—majestic, if lacking something of the three-dimensional relief so fundamental to the classical spirit the artist was seeking to revive. In the exterior of the south wall are immured two interesting pagan spolia: a small piece of a marble sty-lobate (preserving the circular mark of where it formerly supported a column), carved with an inscription and a dolphin; and an attractive, late Hellenistic **grave** *stele*.

On the south side of the square is the **Nautical Muse-um of Kalymnos** (*Open 10–2, except Mon*) an interesting and sometimes moving exhibition of the island's trades and history, and above all of the life and tribulations of the sponge-divers. There are examples of the 'sink-stones' used by the early, naked divers, and of the infamous *skáphandro* diving-suit, which led the divers to go to depths at which they contracted appalling maladies and physiological problems. Early studies and photographs of these diseases are exhibited, as well as the sponges themselves, and the tools and processes used in preparing them for sale and exportation. There is a wealth of fas-cinating photographic documentation. Some of what is exhibited here can be complemented by a visit to a func-tioning **sponge factory**. There are a couple still operat-ing in Póthia, where it is possible to see the processes of cleaning, preparing and grading sponges: one (indicated with signs) lies behind the corner at the west end of the waterfront; another is to the left of the road out to Vathýs, at the eastern side of the port.

SPONGES

Already in Ancient Egypt and in 13th century BC Mesopotamia, sponges, impregnated with opiates and then humidified, appear to have been used for anaesthetising patients during elementary surgery; Roman soldiers carried them to hold lightweight liquid refreshment, and Roman civilians used them as a kind of washable lavatory paper; in Ancient Greece they were kept for bathing and washing; artists of the Renaissance experimented with them in fresco-painting; the Ottoman Sultan's harem ordered them for cosmetic purposes; and potters throughout all these ages have used them as an aid in throwing and finishing a pot. Jesus on the Cross was offered vinegar on a sponge; and defeat is finally conceded by a pugilist when his second 'throws up the sponge'. The properties of sponges lend themselves to all kinds of situations, and their use is as old as history. For millennia, the total world demand for sponges never exceeded the supply guaranteed by the trained bands of sponge-divers who worked in the warm waters of the southeast Aegean—principally around Symi, Chalki, Astypalaia and Kalymnos. Their island waters produced sponges of the very best quality.

The Industrial Revolution changed all that—both the supply and the demand. A rising urban female bourgeoisie in Europe and America developed an insatiable appetite for sponges; at the same time, the development of a deep-water diving suit—the '*skáphandro*'—revolutionised the quantity and whole method of sponge collection. (See '*Sponge-diving*', *under Symi, in vol. 6 of this series*.) The sponge lost its 'specialness' and became an industrially culled commodity; the sponge-diver, too, became little more than an instrument of the productivity locomotive. This undoubtedly brought wealth to the islands which, on Symi and Kalymnos in particular, gave rise to elegant new towns with grand middle-class houses and public buildings. But the boom was to be short-lived: war broke out in 1914; the Italians moved to limit sponge-fishing severely during their occupation of the Islands in the 1920s; the first cheap, synthetic sponges appeared around 1930; a bacterial disease hit Mediterranean sponge beds in 1938; and a gradual awareness grew that the crippling or fatal effects of rapid decompression upon the diver as he rose to the surface in the *skáphandro* had for too long been ignored in the interests of profit and productivity. The industry collapsed, and those whom it supported in the Islands emigrated—mostly to Tarpon Springs, Florida, where they plied the only trade they knew, and set up there what soon were to become the largest sponge farms and factories in the world.

The sponge is an animal—but only just. To the layman it seems like a plant, unable to move and with no muscular, digestive or nervous system. Curiously, however, it can reproduce in two different ways: either by budding and fragmentation, like many plants (for this reason, proper harvesting actually promotes colony-size, rather than depleting it); or it can reproduce sexually, like an animal. Sponges are hermaphroditic, and at certain phases of the moon, release sperm and eggs into the water fertilising one another (not themselves) within a limited colony. They live by pumping water through their internal chambers and filtering out micro-organisms for food. When they are cut, they are exposed to the air to die; all the organic material withers, and the black skin or pellicle which covers its fibres is washed out in a subsequent re-immersion in salt-water. The sponge is then beaten to remove all the dead organic material, and the flexible skeleton (dried and bleached) is what remains for use. 'Wool sponges' are the softest and used for washing and with cosmetics; 'grass sponges' are rougher and are good for painting; the flat-shaped, durable, 'elephant-ear sponges' are those favoured by potters for throwing and finishing. The cycle has now almost come full-circle and natural sponges are sought in small amounts, for specific needs, valued once again for the individual qualities that made them special in Antiquity. These are still harvested by a small fleet based in Kalymnos.

One of Kalymnos's richest and most successful entrepreneurs, and the first to begin wholesale international exportation of sponges, was Nikolaos Vouvalis (1841–1918): the highly decorated and furnished **Vouvalis Mansion**, in the Evanglístria area inland of the north of the water-front, where he lived can still be visited (*open 10–2, except Mon*). It houses a small number of the artefacts destined eventually for the New Archaeological Museum which is being built on the adjacent plot. Only three rooms in the mansion may currently be visited: Vouvalis's study, which exhibits two small 4th century BC marble heads (one male, one female) on his desk; and the dining-room and upstairs drawing-room, which are fascinating for what they show of the prevailing obsession in 19th century Mediterranean bourgeois taste, for highly ornate French, gilt and glass objects, and for chinoiserie. They are further mixed here with the animal-skin rugs and full-length portraits typical of an English country house. There is a marked absence of any point of contact with local culture. Vouvalis, who had been a generous philanthropist to his native island and constructed its first hospital, long pre-deceased his far younger wife, who nonetheless kept in constant touch through a medium with his embalmed corpse in the bedroom, until it finally had to be removed from the building. The garden has a pleasant gazebo covering a scattering of Byzantine stone fragments; near the entrance gates is a collection of pagan altars, architectural fragments and inscriptions, awaiting transfer to the New Museum. One of the centrepieces of the new collection's display will be the important and magnificent **bronze head with hat** (or crown), possibly representing a Hellenistic king, which was recovered from an ancient shipwreck on the sea-bed near Kalymnos in 2002 by a local fisherman. The piece is remarkably well-preserved, with the original glass-paste eyes still in place.

The **area of Evangelístria** around the Vouvalis Mansion contains a vibrant mixture of architectural styles. Small popular houses, built of stone, often with a walled *avlí* (courtyard) and painted in white or a variety of pastel blue and green colours, jostle with larger stone mansions in neoclassical style and more sober ochre colours. A particular speciality of the island is the fine **iron-work** of the balconies, half-moon door-lights, and railings, which, combined with the **carved volutes** and doorframes, lends a lightness and nobility to the buildings. The area takes its name from the **Early Christian basilica of the Evangelístria** at its centre. Only the floor plan of the basilica remains, raised to height of almost 2m on a solid terrace, with a dwarfed modern chapel over its sanctuary area. Below and around the east end are the huge blocks of the podium of the apse: there is similar ashlar-block masonry at the southwest corner which belongs to a preceding pagan building, possibly of the early Classical period.

Detour. At the end of the Bay of Póthia, 2km southwest of the town along the shore-line road, is **Thermá**, a now defunct hydrotherapy spa built during the Italian occupation and refashioned in the 1950s. The natural hot water (37° C) now emerges by the rocks below.

SOUTH OF POTHIA

The main road to Vlichádia (6 km) and the southwest of the island climbs up to the **convent of Aghii Pantes** which is often referred to as 'Aghios Savvás' after the monk, later canonised as a saint, who spent the last 20 years of his life here. Aghios Savvás (1862–1948) has now become the patron saint of the island, though he was born in Thrace. After a period on Mount Athos, he spent almost 10 years as a hermit in the Jordanian desert, and then returned to Greece, where he became a priest at the Holy Trinity convent on Aegina with Nektarios (later Aghios Nektarios), of whom he painted an important icon. He came to Kalymnos in 1927 and lived here at Aghii Pantes, as a spiritual teacher and ascetic, until his death in 1948. The vast convent—almost an independent city—gives today an impression far from the ascetic aspirations of Savvás. The views over Póthia, however, are very fine.

In the village of **Vothíni** (3.5km), to the right of the main road, shortly beyond the turning for the convent, is a **Folklore Museum** and **traditional Kalymniot house** (*open daily 9–3*). The display is informative and well-presented on sponge-fishing, as well as on the customs of marriage and of domestic life on Kalymnos. Samples of traditional Kalymniot wine (similar to port) are offered. Continuing 2.5km further south, on the shore-front at **Vlichádia**, is another 'home-grown' museum, the **Balsamidis Museum of the Sea and Sponge-diving** (*open daily 9–6*), created with considerable dedication and energy by the local diving master, and giving a vivid picture of the variety and interest of the seas around Kalymnos—its fish, shells, sponges, corals, shipwrecks, and buried *amphorae*. It is one man's elaborate paean to the seas.

A number of remains from Early Christian and Roman times are visible in this area. A track uphill and to the south from the opposite side of the road from the Folklore Museum of Vothíni leads (1.7 km southeast) to the isolated **monastery of Aghios Giorgios** built on the site of, and incorporating carved marble elements from, an **Early Christian foundation**, which in turn replaced a place of pagan worship on the panoramic hill-top. At the same site, to the north of the church, is a group of **barrel-vaulted tombs** of the late Roman/Early Christian era. These are a recurring element in the landscape of Kalymnos and of Telendos: three more may be seen just west of the village of Vothíni.

Two kilometres southwest of Vothíni is the **cave of**

Kephála (*open June–Sept daily 10–6*) reached by a newly-made track heading west from the monastery of Aghia Ekaterini, just to the west of the village. This is the most accessible of the many caves on the island: the almost 1,000 sqm area of the cave's six interconnected chambers is entered by a narrow passageway and provides an impressive display of stalactites and stalagmites. It is sometimes referred to as the 'cave of Zeus': this is more a tribute by local tradition to its large size than a reflection of any cult of Zeus which might be suggested by archaeological evidence. Caïques in the harbour of Póthia also offer a service round to the shore below, from which it is a 200m walk up the cave: these trips give the possibility of stopping on the **islet of Nerá** to see the attractive **monastery of the Tímios Stavrós**.

THE VALLEY OF VATHYS

The ideal way to arrive at ***Vathýs** is by boat into its dramatic **fjord-like inlet**, or—failing that—by taking the old flagstone *kalderimi*, rebuilt during the Italian occupation, over the hills northeast of Póthia, which leaves from beside the church of Aghia Triada, not far above the Vouvalis Mansion. It is a shade-less, but panoramic, two-hour walk, passing in the first 20 minutes below the vestigial

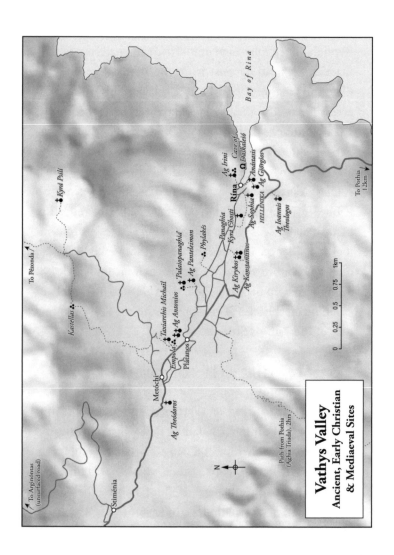

Bay of Rina

To Pothia
12km

Kyrá Panelí

To Pezónda

Kastellas

Taxiárchis Michaíl
Ag Antónios
Emplá
Metóchi
Platános

Ag Theológos

Ag Panteleímon
Palaiopanaghiá

Phylakés
Panaghía
Kyrá Shotí
Rína
Ag Irini
Cave of
Daskaleió
Anastasis
Ag Giorgos

Ag Kirykos
Ag Konstantinos
Ag Sophía
HELLENIKÁ
Ag Ioánnis
Theológos

To Arginóntas
(unsurfaced road)

Stiménia

Path from Pothia
(Aghía Triáda), 2hrs.

N

0   0.25   0.5   0.75   1km

Vathys Valley
Ancient, Early Christian
& Mediaeval Sites

remains of the acropolis (to east) of the ancient settlement of *Póthaia*. But the density of things to be seen in the Vathýs valley unfortunately requires a long time to visit by foot, and so a car or bicycle is all but essential. The asphalt road east of Póthia passes along the scarred and barren south coast of the island: there are fine views to Turkey as it turns north; then the valley of Vathýs suddenly comes into view, paved with intense green vegetation. The intermittent sounds of goat-bells, barking dogs and the crowing of cocks, are a complete contrast to the noise and activity of Póthia. The **valley** has the wide, sculpted form of a glacial glen, but is in fact part alluvial plain and part an inlet of the sea that has silted and remained fertile: it was intensively cultivated in Antiquity, has seen habitation since earliest times, and is unusually rich in **Early Christian remains.**

THE CHURCHES OF THE RINA AREA

A kilometre before reaching the valley-floor, the small 15th century chapel of **Aghios Ioannis Theologos**, is above and to the left of the road on the hillside, built on the foundations of the apse of an earlier 6th century church: the wall-paintings inside are in poor condition— the eyes of the figures abraded and destroyed during the years of the Turkish occupation. Below and to the right (just before the end of the descent) is the church complex of **Aghios Konstantinos**—an open courtyard in which two chapels stand on what was the nave of a large **Early Christian basilica**, with the extensive remains of a 6th century **mosaic floor** of abstract patterns, executed primarily in five colours, visible beside the gate and all along the south side. The south chapel of **Aghios Kirykos** (11th century) has damaged vestiges of 13th century wall-paintings, with some fine faces discernible among the *Saints* on the north and south walls: its threshold is composed of carved marble fragments of the Palaeochristian church. A fine example of an Early Christian public omnibus stands rusting under a tree beyond the eastern end of the site, from where the apse of the 6th century church is visible below the north chapel (erected in 1955). Continuing a little further towards the sea, past burgeoning walled-gardens, you reach the attractive 13th century church of the **Panaghia Kyrá Chostí**, also built inside a larger 6th century predecessor, whose walls, standing to the height at which the vaults spring, are visible to the south side of the existing church, and fragments of which have been used to fashion its window-frames. Two campaigns of **wall-painting** are visible inside: the lower level of the 13th century, and the superimposed patches of the

15th century. The themes are predominantly Marian, beginning with the *Virgin and Child in Majesty* in the conch of the apse.

Rína—a corruption of 'Aghia Irini'—is a tiny harbour, crowded with small fishing boats, perfectly out of sight of the open sea, and protected by its long narrow inlet. In this safe haven a large Early Christian community—known then as *Helleniká*—flourished from the 4th to 7th centuries and covered primarily the north-facing slope to the south of the harbour. The ruins of churches and houses are everywhere on the hillside. Immediately above the water on the south side, is the Early Christian **church of the Anástasis**—its original size deducible from the position of the retaining wall to the south. The church's unusual dedication to the Resurrection is interesting in light of the fact that, from where it stands, the sun is seen to rise over the water at the entrance of the inlet for a substantial period of the year around the equinoxes. Above the church is a cave-like ledge which was cut into the rock, probably in Antiquity. Further above, was the church of **Aghios Giorgios**: the mediaeval chapel on its site preserves vestiges of wall-painting. From here, the dense remains of the main settlement are visible on the hillside to the west, with the vaulted arch of Aghia Sophia conspicuous in the middle. Across the harbour to the north, reached by steps behind the busy boat-yard, is **Aghia Irini**, where a tiny chapel and a rose garden have been built on the north side of the site of a large, apsed basilica of the 5th century, with another ruined basilica, of unknown dedication, beyond to the east. A few pieces of rectangular masonry cut and dressed in typical Hellenistic fashion suggest the pre-existence here of what was perhaps a 4th century BC fort or watch-tower.

At this point you are above and a little to the west of the **cave of Daskaleió** at the north side of the harbour entrance. This can be visited only by boat, either from Rína or from Póthia. It is the island's largest cave, whose importance lies in the finds from Late Neolithic, Minoan and Mycenaean occupation which have been made inside it—among which is a small 17th century BC, Minoan figurine of an adorant in solid bronze, similar in many respects to those found at the mountain-top sanctuary of *Aghios Giorgios sto Vouno* on Kythera and which are now in the Archaeological Museum of Piraeus. Immediately inside the cave is a chamber, about 25m long, from which another, with stalagmites and stalactites and a cavity full of brackish water, opens out (right) at a lower level.

HELLENISTIC AND EARLY CHRISTIAN
REMAINS IN THE CENTRE OF THE VALLEY

Inland of Rína is a network of lanes between high white-washed walls, stately stone houses, and gardens bursting with pomegranate, olive, citrus trees and vines, and punctuated with rose-bushes and cypress. Eight hundred metres in from the harbour-front, to the right of the road on the lower slopes of the hill, just above the line of cultivation, are the remains of a remarkable structure known as '*Phylakés*'. It is constructed of massive rectangular blocks of the local sedimentary stone measuring as much as 190cm x 75cm, which create a chambered structure about 10m x 6m. There is evidence of cutting in the bed-rock in the area behind and to the east side, where more huge blocks are visible. The position is good for surveying the surrounding cultivations, and the walls must represent what remains of a heavily **fortified farmstead** of the late Classical or Hellenistic period, probably endowed with a surveying tower originally. From here, it is possible to cross the fields to the west via the church of Aghios Panteleimon, to the site of the fine, 5th century remains known as '*Palaiopanaghiá*'—though an easier route to it lies by going further inland along the road and to the right at the first junction. There are substantial remains here—

both of the building's lower walls (occasionally plastered and painted), and of the **floor mosaics**. From their simple bold geometric designs, executed in four main colours (two reds, two whites, two blues, and black) these would seem to be the work of the 5th century AD. Where there is no mosaic, there are marble flagstones. The main basilica is a spacious building with three long aisles, once delineated by slender columns (one example in Proconnesian marble lies to the west, adding to the impression of the expensive materials lavished on this early church.) To the north is a large **baptistery** with a cruciform stepped font, clad in marble, sunk into the floor: the base of a *ciborium* can be seen on its east side. A curiosity here lies in the unusual **antechamber** to the baptistery which has a quatrefoil plan and a mosaic floor. The step in the passage between this and the north aisle of the main basilica, is made of a piece of carved, marble *templon* screen from an earlier building, and suggests that this room was added or rebuilt at a later date.

Five hundred metres further to the west is the open square of the village of **Plátanos**, with a café, plane trees and an old water-fountain at the eastern exit of the square. A short distance to its northwest is the valley's richest site—the *****ancient fortress of Empóla** and its **early churches**—which comes into view on top of a low

ridge, accessible by a track to the right of the road. The
rise is crowned by a long stretch of **4th century** BC **walls**
in isodomic masonry composed of rectangular blocks of
a kind of 'pudding-stone', or conglomerate, similar to that
used at Phylakés. The southern stretch, which is encountered first, may have been added in a later enlargement to
the principal area to the north, which includes the sizeable **Hellenistic tower** standing a little to the west of the
Early Christian church. Tracing the lines of the walls in
the surrounding fields gives a sense of the imposing size
of the original 4th century BC structure. The 6th century
AD basilica within it, which incorporates both the ancient
walls at its east end and the ancient tower in its narthex
to the west, is commensurately grand, and once again endowed with clearly patterned **mosaic floors**. The ancient
spolia here are of particular interest and suggest that, in
Antiquity, there may have been more here (a temple, and/
or a cemetery) than just a fortified building: in the curve
of the apse, lies (on its side) the carved marble **doorway
of a Hellenistic monumental tomb** which, perhaps because of the incidental central cross-design created by its
doors, has suggested itself for later Christian use; below
where the *templon* screen would have stood is a long, half-
buried, **section of the entablature** of a sacred building,
with both the triglyphs on the front, and the precise re-

cesses for the metal clips that linked one block to another on the top, still clearly visible. Against the exterior of the whole length of the north wall of the basilica has been added a long narrow vaulted chamber, whose purpose—if not for storage—is obscure. The south aisle of the basilica is today occupied by the 14th century **church of the Taxiarchis Michaïl**, whose simple interior conserves beautiful **wall-paintings**—some of which (the *Pantocrator* and *Evangelists* of the apse) are contemporary with the foundation, and others (the fine *Entry into Jerusalem*, *Nativity*, and *Saints*) date probably from 200 years later.

Two hundred metres to the east of this area, still on the plateau, can be traced the floor-plan of another **6th century church** (dedicated to ?Aghios Demetrios) amongst a quantity of fragments of Antique limestone blocks and Byzantine capitals. The tiny 12th century chapel of **Aghios Antonios** to the south of the modern church has wall-paintings in poor condition in its simple, vaulted chamber.

ABOVE AND AROUND THE VALLEY OF VATHYS

From the western end of Plátanos, the road leads to **Metóchi**; from here, a new track to the north, leads up the mountain-side to the fortified, 18th century **monas-**

tery of Panaghia Kyrá Psilí. (*When the track reaches the watershed at the chapel of Stavrós, a signed foot-path to the right leads on up to the church.*) The dramatically-sited monastery is a votive gift made by a native of the island, who converted to Islam and served as a high official in the Ottoman administration; when a fleet of ships under his management was miraculously rescued from a storm by the intervention of the Virgin, he dedicated and built this monastery on what was probably the site of an earlier hermitage (and of even earlier pagan cult) inside the grottoes where the chapels within the walls now stand. Its hidden and fortified location served as a refuge for the inhabitants of the valley in times of danger.

From Stavrós the pathway to the northeast leads (45 mins each way) down to the island's north shore at the wild and solitary inlet of **Pezónda**. Along the ridge, to the west of Stavrós, at a point where it projects south over the valley in a natural 'acropolis', is a site known as **Kastéllas**: the settlement here, marked by large blocks of collapsed masonry, seems to have been continuously used through the Geometric, Archaic and Classical periods. Jewellery, bronze arrow-heads, coins, and glass vessels have recently been found here.

On leaving the village of Metóchi, this time to the west, the road passes (left) the cemetery church of **Aghios**

Theodoros, which has 16th century wall-paintings in its interior. From here, a wide unpaved track leads further west towards **Stiménia** at the head of the valley, from where it continues (currently under construction) over the bare mountain landscape to the bay of Arginóntas on the island's west coast: the old mule-path, which generally follows the lines of the electricity cables west from the northern end of Metóchi, covers the same distance in a tough, but panoramic, two hour-walk.

CHORIO AND THE NORTH OF THE ISLAND

THE CASTLES AND CHORIO

Between 80–90 per cent of the population of the island lives in the sloping valley between the port of Póthia and Panórmos on the west coast. What was once three or four separate communities has now become an almost continuous band of habitation. The valley is hemmed in by bare limestone slopes to either side, both of which were watched by two sizeable castles to north and south. To the south was the **castle of Chrysocheriá** (*always open: reached by a track to the right of the road to Vlichádia as*

it leaves the southwest corner of Póthia); this is originally a 12th century Byzantine fortress, taken over by the
Knights of Rhodes in the early 1400s and strengthened
by them. The Knights' additions, such as the south tower,
are in a different constructional technique from the earlier Byzantine walls which are typically mortared with
tiles and potsherds between the stones. The prominent
escutcheons are of the Grand Master, Antonio Fluviã
(1421–37) and the frequently encountered, Fantino Que-
rini, Venetian Admiral and Governor of Kos in the 1440s.
The small space enclosed within the walls points to this
having always been more of a look-out and signalling station than a refuge for the population during attack: its
position splendidly commands the whole of the centre
and the port of the island. The 15th century **church of
the Metamorphosis of Christ**—the lower and older of
the two churches within the enceinte—is decorated with
16th century wall-paintings, now in poor condition. Beside its door, a marble block with a clear Hellenistic inscription has been immured, recording a certain '*Nikoda-
mos Ara/togenou, priest at the temple of the Dioscuri*'.

Visible from here on a spur across the valley, opposite and northeast of the Chrysocheriá, is the church of
Aghia Barbara. Inside a **cave** on the hill above the church
were found significant prehistoric remains and objects

from the Late Neolithic and Bronze Age periods. Also clearly visible to the left of this, and almost due north, is the valley's other castle—the extensive fortified area of the Kástro of Chora, occupying the sloping summit of a natural, rock 'acropolis'. This is accessible by a climb up from the centre of Chorió below.

Chorió, or '**Chóra**', was the island's capital until the mid-19th century, founded on a site safely away from the coast and with good natural fortification, during the period of instability and piracy that followed on from the first Arab incursions of the 8th century. Today it is an unpretentious Greek town, free of any jarring tourist paraphernalia. Its narrow streets radiate out from the large central **church of the Panaghia Charitoméni** ('the Gentle Virgin') of 1805. The exterior walls of the church have fragments of the same beautiful decorative frieze of jasmine-flower motif which can also be seen in and around the church of Christ of Jerusalem (*see below*); the interior is dominated by an ornately carved and gilded wooden **iconostasis** bearing several fine 19th century icons.

Streets lead eastwards from the church and uphill to the edge of the habitation, from where a steep and exposed climb on a path across the rocks brings you to the **castle of Chora**, or **Péra Kástro** (*permanently open*) completely encircled by a fine curtain of 15th century walls with wide crenellations, rising directly from the bare rock. Once again, the Knights of Rhodes will have strengthened pre-existing fortifications here, probably in the 15th century—although the presence of the arms of Grand Master del Carretto (1513–21), exhibited prominently on the east walls, suggests that this work may have continued into the next century. The walls rarely exceed a metre in thickness, and the gate here is not built with particular attention to indestructibility: the Kastro was designed first and foremost as a functioning walled city, rather than as a last refuge against siege. Near the entrance inside, you immediately encounter ancient spolia and fragments of marble entablature on the ground, with, nearby, a massive millstone; other ancient pieces (fluted columns and capitals, etc.) are incorporated into the nine small churches on the site which constitute its greatest interest. To the east side, the double-church of the Dormition, attached to the church of Aghios Nikolaos, represents an unusual grouping of forms, including here a short narthex on the south side. To the west, the churches of the **Tímios Stavrós**, of **Aghia Paraskeví**, and of the **Metamorphosis**, have **wall-paintings** of the 16th century and incorporate Ancient and Early Christian spolia in their fabric. At the top of the enclosure is the greatest concentration of stone houses that have preserved their walls to a reasonable height, most built over deep water-cisterns. The few larger public buildings are all of a functional, four-square, military design; one of them preserves a conspicuous escutcheon, with a Frankish coat of arms, on its south wall.

At the western extremity of Chorió, on the main road to Pánormos, is the town's cemetery, whose entrance is dominated by the 7m high **sculpture of *Christ Crucified*** by the Kalymniot sculptor, Michalis Kokkinos: the torso and head have an expressive quality, which is somehow lost in the less carefully conceived arms and legs. To the south from here, a road leads up to the airport and to the plateau of Argos.

Detour to Argos. **Argos**—whose name (found also on Nisyros and Rhodes) recalls Herodotus's comment (*Hist.* V11. 99) that the earliest settlers of these islands were Dorians from the area of the Argolid in the Peloponnese—is a scattered settlement across a high, semi-fertile plateau at c. 170m above sea-level: the virtue of the site lay in the security afforded by its inaccessibility and invisibility from the sea. The plateau was reached in Antiquity by a **stone path and stairway** of which traces are still visible near the church of the Tris Gerarches: today a steep, paved road climbs up the scarp, and leads up to the island's dramatically sited air-strip. Beside the turning for the **airport** at the top of the ascent are the 11th century **church of the Aghii Apostoli** (lower church) and the 13th century **church of the Panaghia Kyrá**, which together form a monastic dependency of the Monastery of St John on Patmos, whose founder, Hosios Christódoulos (*see pp. 117–9*), is said also to have founded the earlier of the two churches here. The many ancient fragments and spolia that have been incorporated into the structure point to a pre-existing pagan sanctuary here as well. The interior has undergone conservation work and patches of 12th century wall-paintings, still with some areas of rich colour along the north wall, are preserved. The **views** on descending from Argos are comprehensive—across to Péra Kástro, whose stone walls and buildings are perfectly camouflaged against the rocky mountainside behind, and down to Póthia, with the coast of Turkey beyond, and the sharp, table-top rock of the Castle of Chrysocheriá to the right of the field of vision. (*End of detour.*)

THE SANCTUARY OF APOLLO AND THE CHURCHES OF CHRIST OF JERUSALEM AND AGHIA SOPHIA

Less than 1km from Chorió, along the main road to Panórmos, almost on the watershed of the sloping valley, is

the site of the island's most important centre of cult in
Antiquity, the **sanctuary of Apollo Dalios** (a Doric vari-
ant of *Δήλιος*, 'Delian'). In the Early Christian period two
basilicas were built over the sanctuary, one of which,
known as the church of Christ of Jerusalem, incorporates
a mass of important ancient inscriptions and architectural elements in its construction. These were observed
by Charles Newton as early as 1854/5 on his visit to the
island; he removed a number of them that were lying in
the area and brought them back to the British Museum
in London. The site was more systematically uncovered
by the Italians in 1937, and ongoing excavations by the
Greek archaeological authorities are bringing to light new
material each year. Two colossal cult statues of Asklepios
and Hygieia, have been found in recent years, as well as a
fine, dressed *kouros* of the 6th century BC.

The ancient temple of Apollo was surrounded by a
dense grove of sacred bay-trees; the visitor needs to imag-
ine, in lieu of today's sounds of traffic from the road, the
vibrant chatter of birds in these trees, especially at sun-
rise and sunset—moments particularly sacred to Apollo,
as divinity of the sun's light. There was a small theatre,
where competitions of song and music were held; and the
sanctuary would have been thronged with votive sculptures, especially in the form of *kouroi*—sculptures of

young men (mostly nude), as if in the likeness of Apollo himself. The **base of the temple** is visible to the south of the standing apse of the church of Christ of Jerusalem, below the line of the subsidiary road. Once again there is a conscious variety of colours of stone used in the buildings being uncovered here. This was probably a 4th century BC building, even though the cult of Apollo here goes back to the 7th century BC and carried on through into Roman times. It would have been a small tetrastyle Ionic temple; parts of an entablature with carved triglyphs, and fluted columns, near the ruined apse almost certainly belonged to it—as did also the fragments of a **fine cornice with deep dentils** on the rear exterior of the apse. The building was oriented north/south, which is unusual for a dedication to Apollo: these mostly faced east—even though the great temple of Apollo *Epikourios* at Bassae is another notable exception.

The huge standing central apse of the basilica of ***Christ of Jerusalem** is one of the most evocative Early Christian remains in the Greek Islands, giving a rare feel for the size and majesty of these strangely heterogeneous buildings—part brick, part stone, assembled from randomly compiled elements, pulled down from pagan predecessors. Here the seats of the *synthronon* in the apse are adapted from those of the ancient theatre, and the

walls and the floor are composed of **inscribed** *stelai* and
pieces of entablature, some mounted sideways, some up-
side down, some religious in character (e.g. the beautiful
inscription mentioning the **dedication** to Apollo *Dalios*, on the north side), some political in nature (e.g. the
public decrees, citizen lists, arbitration texts and dedications of different periods, to the south side), some purely
decorative (e.g. the running, tendrilled flower motif on
the projections to both sides)—all jumbled together with
imperious indifference. The church's long nave, which
would have extended west of the apse, was flanked by
fluted columns separating the space of the aisles to north
and south, and roofed with wooden beams and terracotta tiles. Legend holds that the church's foundation goes
back to the visit of the Emperor Arcadius (395–408) on
his way back to Byzantium from Jerusalem: the building's
grandeur would certainly suggest a founder of such importance.

Fifty metres to the east of the apse—across an area of
chicken-coops and heaped ancient fragments—are excavations which are revealing the **mosaic floors** and walls of
another Late Roman or Palaeochristian building, referred
to either as the **Basilica of the Evangelístria** or of **Aghia
Sophia**. The mosaics are mostly in the bold abstract designs typical of the late 5th and early 6th centuries; those

in the long west 'narthex' are distinguished by their depictions of fish, camels, mythological beasts and plants, similar in style and execution to those at Nimboreio on Symi. The exact form of the building remains problematic until more of it is excavated: the presence of an unusual semicircular 'apse' in the middle of the south wall suggests that it had no ordinary basilica form. Currently, there are the low walls of a small chapel (Aghia Sophia), hastily erected from a mixture of rubble and large, rusticated ancient blocks over the main eastern apse, with the marble base of the original *templon* screen visible inside. Buildings here have clearly been raised and destroyed more than once, and, until the northern side is revealed by excavation, the overall history and nature of the site remain obscure.

Tombs from Hellenistic and Roman times, often with precious or informative grave goods, have been found widely in the area of this valley, while on the slopes of the hill opposite the sanctuary of Apollo to the north, on a rise between two ravines, are excavations revealing the **Hellenistic settlement of Damos**, where residential *insulae* and stepped streets are currently being uncovered. Further west, towards Panórmos, and northeast of the church of Aghios Antonios, have been discovered late **Roman thermae**.

KANTOUNI, PANORMOS AND MYRTIES

The main road to the north, now a tree-lined avenue, descends after passing the church of Christ of Jerusalem to a junction (4.5 km from Póthia), where a left branch-road leads to **Linária** and **Kantoúni**, two contiguous villages with attractive houses and gardens overlooking an intimate west-facing bay with sandy beaches. From Kantoúni there are footpaths leading to the panoramic **monastery of Stavroú**, and further west (40 minutes) to the more remote monastery of Aghia Photiní. 'ature**Panórmos**'—which also has an attractive beach, Platýs Yialós—refers more to an area than a particular centre, and covers the scattered community of houses and gardens on the lower west-facing slopes of Mount Prophítis Elías, which rises to the island's highest peak (676m) behind. Before the main road begins to descend steeply to the coast at Myrtiés, with striking views across to Telendos, a sign indicates a left turn to the **Early Christian basilica of Aghios Ioannis** at Melitsácha: it possibly occupies what was the panoramic site of a temple of Poseidon. Once again it is the fine **mosaics**—clear, confident and well-ordered in design, and with a **dedicatory inscription** of a certain '*Anatolios*'—which are the site's greatest joy. By comparison with the other Palaeochristian buildings on the island, this is of smaller scale: the marble pillars of the nave with their **carved panels** closing off the north aisle are still in place at points, and the base of the *templon* screen, the *synthronon* and marble floor of the sanctuary are all clearly visible; their colour contrasts with the black volcanic threshold-stone of the west doorway. A modern funerary chapel occupies the southeast corner, and there are the remains of an 11th century chapel to the south. From here, the road descends steeply to **Myrtiés**, the harbour both for the regular shuttle-boats to Telendos (*see next section*), and for the daily ferry, which sails through the dramatic bay of Arginónta, and round the northern point of the island to Xerókambos on Leros.

THE NORTH OF THE ISLAND

To the north of Myrtiés, the coastal strip as far as **Masoúri**, and a little beyond, is dedicated to seasonal tourism. Seawards, it is dominated by the imposing profile of Telendos across the water; landwards, it is backed by dramatic mountains which, to the north of Masoúri, drop in vertical rock-faces below their summits, perforated with caves and overhangs. These are a rock-climber's paradise—a sport for which Kalymnos is becoming increasingly well-known. Information may be had from the Municipal

Athletics Organisation's Climbing Information Desk (*T 22430 59445; e-mail mao@Klm.forthnet.gr or jckalymn@ ath.forthnet.gr*) which is situated in Masoúri (9 km from Póthia). At 10.5 km the road passes **Kastélli**—a projecting conical headland crowned by an eroded knob of rock, where there are the remains of a Byzantine fortress of the 7th century AD. The site is dramatic (especially at sunset) and looks across to the towering profile of Telendos, with its contemporaneous settlement of Aghios Konstantinos directly opposite. The steep slopes have substantial remains of stone houses, rock-cut cisterns and thick scatters of potsherds and broken tiles; stretches of the multiple defensive walls are traceable—an inner ring at the summit and a main enceinte with towers below, as well as a steep run of walls down to the shore in the middle of the south slope. Though the slopes are barren now, they would once have been consolidated in terraces with dwellings, and green with plants and trees in between.

The deep cut into the coast of the **bay of Arginónta** constitutes another half-amphitheatre of mountainous rock-faces with many impressive caves, at the head of which, in a rare oasis of green, is the village of Arginónta (19km). From here, tracks lead southeast over the pass to Metóchi and into the Valley of Vathýs. At **Skália**, 4km north of Arginónta, are a number of points of interest:

above the village, the church of **Aghios Mamás**—reached by a stone path and steps up from the tiny *plateia*—is built on the base of an ancient building; below, at the shore, the whitewashed, cemetery church of **Aghios Nikolaos** is built into the remains of a large **Early Christian basilica** of the 6th century, whose well-preserved north wall still towers above the more recent church. In the interior are patches of 14th century wall-painting (north side), beside a framed icon of St Nicholas, festooned with sponges. From Skália, a rough track climbs over the barren ridge and down to the northeast coast at the **bay of Palaiónisos**, where a community of half a dozen souls and their goats survive, by a small shingle beach.

The finest archaeological remains in this sector of the island are the ruins of the ****Hellenistic fortress of Kastrí**—the brilliant and almost invisible fortification of a cleft in the mountainside, which commands some of the most stunning views in the area. The site is well-camouflaged, and nestles about half-way below the summit of the rock face to the north of the last sharp bend in the road before the settlement of Emboreió begins. From the house and goat-pens just above the road, a path—vestigially marked with red spots—leads directly up the mountain, first to the right of the torrent-course, and then to the left, until the roughly rectangular hewn blocks of the construction come into view below the rock face. The ascent is steep, rocky and takes the full sun. The site consists of a **curtain wall** in polygonal masonry which links two small **rectangular towers** (c. 3.5m. square) on rocky spurs to either side, and seals off a natural cleft in the rock face: below are rock-cut steps and a **doorway** hewn through the rock, with the fixtures for the gate cut into its surface. This leads steeply up to the east side and onto a rock ledge, where there is a plastered cistern, again carved from the living rock. Beyond it lies a neatly **carved olive-press stone**, with clear-cut channels for the outflow of the oil. (Further to the west of Kastrí, below the ridge, are the remains of what appears to be an ancient olive-press installation.) To this day, the site feels very safe: it must always have been an impregnable refuge which dominated the land and water routes, and the islet of Kalavrós below. The *view is magnificent, and it should be recalled that if, when this structure was built in the 5th or 4th century BC, Telendos was still, as some claim, a headland attached to the mainland, there would then have been no open channel to the south (*see 'The Earthquake of 554 AD', below*).

The fortress at Kastrí would have protected, and served as an acropolis for, the ancient settlement of **Emboreió**, which, though a sleepy, end-of-the-road village today, must once have been a flourishing centre, if its ancient name '*Empórion*' ('trading station') is anything to go by. Systematic excavation has not been undertaken here, but there are ancient blocks incorporated into walls of buildings and fields in this area, and the ground is richly scattered with potsherds in places. The church of **Aghios Giorgios** is built on the ruins of an Early Christian predecessor; and the few remains of **Late Roman** *thermae* can be seen by the shore at the east end of the bay. Prominently visible on the hillside above and to the east of Emboreió, is a large stone-built barn-like construction, probably dating from the around the 6th century AD and generally referred to as the '*Evryótholos*' (or 'wide-vaulted building'). A church it clearly never was. Its form—a long barrel-vaulted single chamber, buttressed by thick walls on the long sides—is not unlike a large version of the tombs found all over Telendos (*see below*). But this would be an unusually large example; it may therefore share more in common with the granaries and storage-barn *tholoi*, encountered, for example, on the islands of Agathonisi, and Pharmakonisi (*see pp. 178–9*), which lie not far to the north of Kalymnos.

TELENDOS

Small boats from Myrtiés cross the channel to ***Telendos** every 30 minutes (15 minute crossing) and arrive at a peaceful waterfront of cafés, tavernas and supply-shops, undisturbed by the sounds and movement of motorized traffic. It is possible and delightful to stay on the island (*see 'Lodging' below*); the walking, swimming and bird-watching are all good, in addition to the interest provided by the quantity of **Early Christian remains**.

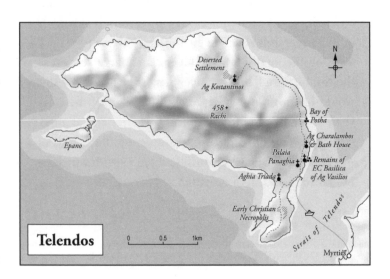

THE EARTHQUAKE OF 554 AD

A popular tradition, repeated unquestioningly in recent years from one source to the next, holds that Telendos was joined to the main body of Kalymnos until the catastrophic earthquake of 554 AD caused the low land to its east to subside under the water, leaving Telendos as a separated island. Something similar—albeit on a smaller scale—happened with the island of Elafonisos after the earthquake of 375 AD. It is true that foundations of small buildings may be seen underwater in the vicinity of the harbour, as well as at points along the eastern shore. It is probably these remains that have given rise to the persistent legend both of a 'lost city' beneath the water, and of a Telendos joined to the main island less than 2,000 years ago. There is no doubt that the earthquake of 554 was especially powerful; the destruction it caused was felt in Constantinople, and is evident on the coast of Asia Minor and in many of the neighbouring islands—especially Kos. The seismic shocks are said to have continued intermittently for two weeks. But earthquakes, unlike volcanic eruptions, only rarely cause large-scale land-subsidence. The strait of Telendos is 750–800m wide, and an average 10m in depth at its deepest point; at a conservative guess, any spit of land that joined the headland to the opposite shore must have been 60–100m wide and at least 5m above sea level. The earthquake would have had to have been of sufficient force to sink more than 45,000sq m of land with a fall of 15m in depth; and this would probably only have been achieved by some degree of subsidence of the whole rock structure of Telendos. It is clear that both the acute effects of the earthquake and the chronic effects of slow subsidence over the centuries, have caused the shoreline to advance several dozen metres in-land over what was a low lying and inhabited area that ringed the island. But in the absence both of a reliable original source for this extraordinary event, and of archaeological evidence or references in inscriptions which help to corroborate it, caution is needed in assuming that a single geological anomaly on this scale occurred without leaving further physical evidence over the general area of the southeast Aegean.

From the landing quay, a path in to the village and to the left (south), leads past the modern church of the Zoödochos Pigi, whose altar is composed of a piece of ancient column surmounted by a capital. It continues up to a rise behind, above the beach of Chochlakás which faces west. The foundations of the early 6th century **church of Aghia Triada** are to the right. Inside a broad basilica-plan with three apses, and a further apsed *parecclesion* along the south side, can be seen the base of a *ciborium*, fragments of capitals, and traces of a fine **marble inlay floor** in the nave. From here the path leads downhill and south, through pine-trees, to the area of the **Early Christian necropolis**, where a number of the **funerary chapels** still stand in varying degrees of ruin. The beginnings of pendentives in the corners of the square chapel in this group show that it was originally a domed structure, of a form similar to a '*martyrion*'. The others vary considerably in size, but most have a widely-vaulted interior and a low shelf of stone around the interior walls, under which the burial *loculi* were organised. These constructions again date from the 6th century AD.

The path to the right of the landing-quay, which leads back into the settlement, turns toward the north and passes the site of the early church of **Palaiá Panaghiá**, which is at the centre of a large number of collapsed dwellings on all sides. The central apse (one originally of three) is in front of you as you climb the path, constructed in poorer material and technique than many of the surrounding churches. Just beyond it, in an open space, is the massive **Early Christian basilica of Aghios Vasílios**. At 40m long by 25m wide and still standing to a height of nearly 8m in places, this is the largest and best preserved Early Christian structure on the two islands. An earthquake of the magnitude of that of 554 AD would have left little here standing, and it is possible that the walls we see now were re-erected after it in the late 6th century: in fact there are clearly two different periods of construction, with the predominantly redder stone used in the lowest courses of the main apse and in the south east corner (pre-554), predating the walls above which may be from a hastier rebuilding after the earthquake. The large finely-cut blocks in the corners used for strengthening appear to have been taken from an earlier pagan construction: other marble blocks, some carved with Byzantine crosses, lie around or have been incorporated as architraves etc. The basilica had additional rooms along the south side (in similar fashion to the basilica at Mastichari on Kos)—one of them (southeast corner), originally domed and with vestiges of plaster and red paint still visible. There are two **funerary chambers** in the vicinity, one at the northwest corner of the narthex, the other just south of the complex. Between the church and the shore, are the remains of a contemporaneous **bath-house chamber** which also incorporates ancient stones. The surrounding area is covered with the remains of houses and other buildings of the Palaeochristian period. At the northern extremity of the settlement and set back a little from the shore is the tiny 13th century **church of Aghios Charalambos**, built into the ruins of another **Early Christian bath-house**, whose succession of interconnected and once vaulted chambers adjoin it to the north.

From here, the path continues along the shore and then climbs over rocks, passing at one point a huge dark stone block, cut so as to function as a counterweight in an olive-press and surviving from an ancient mill, now vanished, on this site. At the base of a small promontory separating the bay of Pótha from the next cove to the north (referred to as '*Paradise Bay*' by its largely nudist clientele) are the vestigial remains of another Early Christian church with **foundations partly submerged** in the sea. It is from here that a rough and stony path (marked initially by faded white and blue paint-spots) leads steeply from the shore round to the north side of the island and climbs to the *deserted settlement and church of Aghios Konstantinos** (1 hour each way). Spread over a ledge at an altitude of 170m, with a dominating escarpment above which

rises to a summit of 458m, and with sweeping views of
the mountains and Bay of Arginónta in front, the setting
here takes its place, with Palaiochora on Kythera and with
Kastro on Skiathos, amongst the most dramatic Byzantine
sites in the islands: but the remains are less well-preserved
here because the site is substantially older than either of
the other two. With the beginning of hostile incursions
into the Southeast Aegean in the late 7th century AD, the
inhabitants of the island sought protection in this inaccessible refuge; the settlement appears later to have been
abandoned in the 10th century. It was protected on the
north side by **walls**, with a protruding rampart below
what must have been a watchtower in the centre. Plastered
cisterns, which are to be seen all around, constituted the
foundations of the houses which rose on top of them. On
a rock outcrop at the eastern extremity is the **church of
Aghii Konstantinos and Eleni**, built inside the surviving
apse of its predecessor of the 7th century and still preserving patches of some **original painting** on its ceiling.
The cut-stone arch of the apse is particularly fine. The
over-riding reason for making the difficult journey here,
however, is for the **setting**, and for the vivid sense that the
site gives of the material privations and the spiritual and
aesthetic rewards of life in these remote refuges from the
violent insecurity of the world of the early Dark Ages.

PRACTICAL INFORMATION

85 200 **Kalymnos**: area 110sq km; perimeter 96km; population 15,706; max. altitude 676m. **Port Authority**: T. 22430 24444. **Travel and information**: Kalymnos Municpality, www.kalymnos-isl.gr; Magos Travel, T. 22430 28777.

ACCESS

By air: Kalymnos now has a small and dramatically sited airport at a distance of 5.5km from Póthia, served by Olympic Air, providing connections with Athens five times a week, mostly with a stop en route at Astypalaia.

By boat: There are daily services by catamaran (*Dodecanese Express*), and four times weekly by car ferry (*F/B Nisos Kalymnos*), south to Kos, and north to Leros, Patmos (&

Samos—ferry only). There are daily boats to Piraeus and to Rhodes, operated by GA Ferries, making also twice weekly stops at Tilos, Nisyros and Symi on the way to Rhodes. The faster *Flying Dolphin* services link Kalymnos (Póthia) also with the smaller Dodecanese Islands between Samos in the north and Rhodes in the south, and run daily in summer. There are daily services in summer (only intermittently out of season) between Póthia and Pserimos, and between Myrtiés and Xerókambos on Leros, weather permitting.

LODGING

For character and tranquillity, **Villa Themelina* is the most congenial place to stay in Póthia (*T. 22430 22682, 23920 email: antoniosantonoglu@yahoo.de*). It is a Belle Epoque, family mansion, with high-ceilinged rooms (and some newer studio rooms around the swimming pool), run by the hospitable owners in a quiet area close to the museum. With more straightforward facilities, and a good view of the town, is the **Hotel Panorama** (*T. 22430 23138, 22917; www. panorama-kalymnos.gr*). For beach-side accommodation

in Kantouni Bay, on the west of the island, **Koletti Studios** are in a delightful setting (*T. 22430 47922, or, out of season, 210 692.8909*); and the tiny shore-side guest-house, **On the Rocks**, facing Kalymnos from Telendos (*T. 22430 48260, 48261; www.otr.telendos.com*) is perfect for a peaceful retreat.

EATING

The taverna **'Pandelis'**, in a tiny square directly behind the **Olympic Hotel** on the waterfront, does not have a wide choice, but what is offered is prepared well—with care and attention to freshness, lightness and flavour. The ouzeri **'Sphoungaras'**, in an alley behind the Emporiki Bank (where Patr. Maximou

Street meets the promenade) has excellent *mezé*, and is crowded with locals at lunchtime. Around the island— both '**Popy's**' at Vathýs, and '**Akti**' in a delightful setting at Emboreió, are good for fresh fish dishes.

FURTHER READING

On the sponge trade: *Bitter Sea: The Real Story of Greek Sponge Diving*, by Faith Warn (2000); and, *The Bellstone: Greek Sponge Divers of the Aegean*, by Michael Kalafatas (2003).

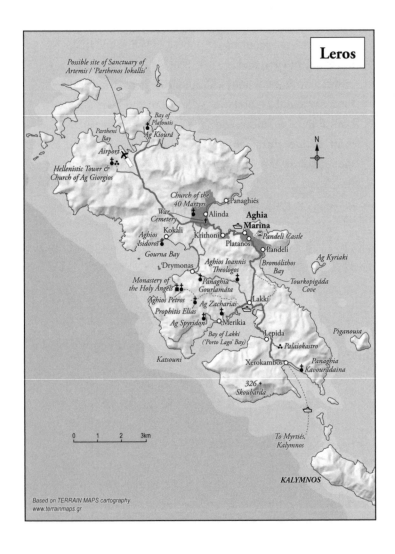

Leros

Possible site of Sanctuary of
Artemis / 'Parthenos Iokallis'

Bay of
Plafoutis

Ag Kioura

Partheni
Bay

Airport

Hellenistic Tower &
Church of Ag Giorgios

N

Church of the
40 Martyrs   Panaghiés

War   Alinda   **Aghia**
Cemetery   **Marina**

Aghios   Kokali   Krithoni   Pandeli Castle
Isidoros   Platanos
Gourna Bay   Pandeli   Ag Kyriaki

Drymonas   Aghios Ioannis   Bromólithos
Theologos   Bay
Monastery of   Panaghia   Tourkopigáda
the Holy Angels Gourlamáta   Cove
Aghios Petros   Ag Zacharias   Lakkí
Prophitis Elias
Ag Spyridon   Merikia
Bay of Lakkí   Lepida   Piganousa
('Porto Lago' Bay)   Palaiokastro
Katsouni
Xerokambos   Panaghia
Kavourádaina

326
Skoubárda

0   1   2   3km

To Myrtiés,
Kalymnos

KALYMNOS

Based on TERRAIN MAPS cartography.
www.terrainmaps.gr

LEROS

Leros has peacefulness, beauty and a wide variety of interest for its modest size. These qualities have for long passed unnoticed because of a number of preconceptions stemming from the recent history of the island which have tended to cloud its image. As a large naval and military base for the Italian occupation during the years between the wars; as a place of exile and reclusion for political prisoners under the Colonels' Junta; and as a centre for a series of mental institutions and hospitals that have been the object of shaming criticisms of misconduct and inhumanity in the last 20 years, Leros still struggles hard to overcome a dark reputation. It is therefore all the more surprising to discover that it is such a radiant and gracious island—a coastline of magnificent bays, a handsome *chora* dominated by a dramatic castle, a number of interesting museums, early rural churches, and villages that burst with flowers and trees amidst a landscape of rocky hills. Extraordinary and unforgettable, is the island's principal harbour, Lakkí—an evocative assemblage of architectural forms and ideas, created in one of the most complete examples anywhere of so-called 'Futurist' or 'Rationalist' planning. What it evokes—Italy's imperial aspirations between the Wars—may not delight, but its historical and aesthetic interest cannot be denied. Although now rather ruined and neglected, the wide sweep of buildings on the harbour's waterfront, from Elementary School to Customs House, is worth the visit to Leros alone to see.

Leros feels like, and is, a compact island, and its short distances can be covered easily on foot. With a deeply indented coastline, varied vegetation, and a stimulating combination of different kinds of architecture, there is always considerable visual interest, and little real ugliness, on the island. Its Ancient and Early Christian remains, whose effect depends more on setting than on content, are largely undramatic, while monuments from an unexpectedly different quarter can sometimes speak more eloquently: the unique murals by political exiles of Greece's Military Junta in the late sixties in the remote chapel of Aghia Kiourá, are a good example. Leros rewards exploration that is unhurried and, above all, open-minded.

HISTORY

Two of the island's many sheltered bays have so far yielded substantial evidence of prehistoric settlement and trade of the 4th millennium BC. Finds of obsidian, of a kind that comes from both nearby Gialí (Nisyros), and of a purer form from Milos in the Western Aegean, show that the material was fashioned in workshops on Leros (in the area of Drymónas) and that there was therefore frequent long-distance trade by sea between these islands in this early period. Little trace of Minoan or Mycenean artefacts has been found, however, even though there was a significant Minoan trading presence at Miletus on the coast opposite.

In early historic times Leros was an Ionian island whereas Kalymnos, and its southern neighbours as far as Rhodes, were Dorian. Leros and Kalymnos almost touch and are even referred to by the same general name—the 'Calydnian Islands'—by Homer in the *Iliad*; but their histories and cultures are separate. Leros was influenced by, fortified by, written about by, and settled by people from Miletus, one of the greatest of the Ionian cities in the 6th century BC. Phokylides of Miletus, a poet of this period, refers to the island somewhat derisorily in an epigram; and Herodotus, in talking about the Ionian revolt of 498

BC (*Hist.* V. 125), mentions that Leros was suggested to Aristagoras, Tyrant of Miletus, as a safe refuge which it was worth his fortifying well, against the possibility of his being forced to flee from Miletus. Athenian tribute lists of 454/453 BC also refer to Milesians 'from Leros'. By the 4th century BC, Leros appears as a deme of Miletus. The 6th century BC philosopher, Demodikos, and the later Hellenistic historian, Pherekydes, were both from Leros: the latter's history of the island is lost, depriving us of valuable information on the subject. The main settlement on the island in Antiquity—continuously inhabited from Geometric through to Roman and Early Christian times—was at the southeast corner of Alinda Bay; the principal religious centre was the sanctuary of Artemis, or *Parthenos Iokallis*, in Parthéni Bay. Early Christian basilicas were built at both of these sites as well as at several other places on the island attesting to a large and well-established Christian community. A bishop of Leros is first mentioned as present at the Fifth Ecumenical Council of Constantinople in 553 AD.

Against opposition from the islanders, the fertile lands at Teménia (east of Lakkí) and around Parthéni, and a portion of the fortress of Pandéli, were all given by the Byzantine Emperor, Alexius I Comnenus, in 1088 to Hosios Christódoulos to be a revenue for the monastery of St John on Patmos. Together with Rhodes and Kos, Leros was acquired by the Knights of St John in 1306, who strengthened and considerably enlarged the existing Byzantine castle in the course of the next century. In 1522 it became a Turkish possession after the defeat of the Knights of Rhodes by the Ottoman Sultan, Suleiman the Magnificent. It was taken briefly by the Venetian Admiral, Leonardo Foscolo, in 1648 during hostilities between Turkey and Venice.

Leros generally enjoyed a measure of independence under Ottoman rule; this gave it the possibility to participate actively in the War of Independence in 1821; in 1830 it briefly had a local Greek Governor as part of the new Greek State, but returned under Ottoman rule again through the terms of the London Protocol of the same year. In the following decades of the 19th century, there was an important and rich community of intellectuals and businessmen who had emigrated to Egypt from Leros, and who were to become important benefactors of the island's architecture, art collections, schools and institutions. During the Italian Occupation of the Dodecanese (1912–43) Leros was transformed by the *avant-garde* building projects of the new 'Porto Lago' (Lakkí) area. The island was the scene of fierce fighting in the Second World War, culminating in the Battle of Leros in November 1943 (*see below*), when it was taken by German forces. It joined the Greek State in 1948 together with all the Dodecanese Islands. The substantial legacy of military buildings on Leros was used for confining political prisoners during the period of the Colonels' Junta (1967–74), and thereafter others were used as a National Mental Institution. Between 1989 and 1995 this was the object of a European Union inquest into maladministration of funds and maltreatment of patients. Substantial improvements in conditions and the opening of a large nursing school in 1999 have helped to put the worst period behind.

The guide to the island has been divided into two sections:
- *Lakkí and the south and west of the island*
- *Aghia Marina and the north of the island*

LAKKI &
THE SOUTH & WEST OF THE ISLAND

LAKKI

When the sea is rough, entry through the narrow opening (less than 400m across) into **Porto Lago Bay**, today's *Ormos Lakkíou*, is a dramatic relief. Always calm, this very large, natural harbour in the southwest of the island was coincidentally well-named by the Italians 'Port Lake'— even though the name was actually given in honour of the first Italian Governor of the Dodecanese, Mario Lago. It is relatively deep on its south side where the naval installations are, and shallower and sunnier on the north side where the city was laid out. *Lakkí, as the port and town are now called, which was created between 1934 and 1938, is unlike anything else in Greece: one would expect to find it more likely in the Pontine plains south of Rome. It constitutes the most coherent and complete example of so-called 'Rationalist' planning and architecture in the Eastern Mediterranean. Its broad streets and open squares, however, desperately lack that narrow intimacy that is so habitual in a Greek town; they seem like ill-fitting clothes on today's inhabitants and shop-keepers.

LAKKI AND THE ITALIAN URBAN PLAN OF 1934

The large ancient towns of Kos and Rhodes offered the Italians little scope for laying out a new town from scratch, but in the empty spaces around this bay there was ample possibility to give architectural form to the political and cultural pretensions that lay behind Italy's occupation of the Dodecanese Islands. The military base in the area of Lépida on the south shore of the bay came first (the 'G. Rossetti Air Base' of 1923); this grew into the largest military base in the Eastern Mediterranean, and included a number of residences and buildings for military administration and housing laid out with gardens, which are now the core of the *Leros National Sanatorium*. Growing needs for housing and entertainment for the officers and their families led the authorities to expropriate land and create the new town of '*Porto Lago*' in 1934—today's Lakkí—which was designed to meet the civilian needs of a military community of about 7,500 people. The architects of the plan were Rodolfo Petracco and Armando Bernabiti, who had already been deeply involved in the master-plans for Rhodes and Kos (*see vols 2 & 6 in this series*). The style here on

Leros represents a half-way house between the more whimsical work of Florestano di Fausto (often called 'Integrationist' because of its aspiration to combine local traditions in architecture together with a new 'Rationalist' approach) seen in the early Italian buildings of the 1920s on Kos and Rhodes, and the heavier and more rigorously 'purified' forms (typified by the Theatre and *Demarcheion* in Rhodes) which began to dominate in the later years of Fascism. The forms of the architecture here are simple and comprehensible, creating a constant play between symmetry and asymmetry, and between regular and irregular forms. Above all else, the spirit of the design lies in 'streamlined' buildings; they seem to intimate a future world of machine-oriented orderliness. The lines are clear and clean, and the volumes full and satisfying. In the predominantly white cubic forms, flat roofs and brightly coloured detailing of these buildings there is still an obvious connection with the local, vernacular architecture of the islands.

The **street plan** of the town is not a regimented grid-pattern, but a rounded and decentralised design, which sympathetically absorbs and reflects the natural curve of the shoreline. Nor are the shapes and volumes of the buildings drearily regular, symmetrical or predictable, but are scattered spatially and alternate between rounded and rectangular forms. In and around the centre of the promenade are the bold circular tower of the former **town hall**, the long horizontal form of the **Hotel Roma** (later called the *Leros Palace Hotel*, and currently in a condition almost beyond salvation), the semicircular projecting foyer of the **theatre** (all by Armando Bernabiti), the sharp vertical of the **clock tower** (set at an interestingly obtuse angle to the building from which it rises) beside the low, half-domed circle-in-a-square of the **food market** with its airy internal peristyle (both by Rodolfo Petracco); further east is the curving façade of the **commercial building** which occupies the next block (note the herring-bone decoration of the upper floor on the southeast corner), and finally the arcaded front of the *****Elementary School** (Petracco) at the eastern extremity, which repeats and synthesises all these shapes in what is certainly the most interesting design of the whole complex. The administrative buildings that frame the town to the sides are deliberately more rectilinear; and in the spacious plots behind, are warehouses, barracks, hospital buildings, the **church of St Francis** (now of Aghios Nikolaos) by Bernabiti, and many **private houses** built for the non-commissioned officers—no two the same, and each one an experiment in a new inversion or combination of the familiar forms. Everywhere, too, the Italians had the sense to plant trees in abundance.

The setting of this architecture and the **bay of Lakkí** are beautiful; the wideness of the lagoon complements the low spaciousness of the town, and the flat, fertile land around sets off the play of its geometrical shapes. Today, a number of memorials and **war monuments** punctuate the townscape: those on the waterfront commemorate a defining moment in the Dodecanese Campaign of 1943—the sinking by the German Air Force of the Greek destroyer *Vasílissa Olga*, and (on the road south to Lépida) of the British destroyer HMS *Intrepid*, both on 26 September 1943—which opened the way to the eventual capture of the island by German forces on 16th November 1943 (*see Battle of Leros, below*). A few blocks inland from the shore, in Plateía Eleftherías, is a monument to a figure who fought for the independence and freedom from occupation of the Dodecanese, Paris Roussos (1875–1966).

Looking west-southwest from the waterfront, the distant island of Levitha (Ancient *Lebinthos*) can be seen distantly through the centre of the narrow entrance of the bay.

LAKKI TO KATSOUNI

(*Southwest, 4km*)

The road which climbs over the rise above the ferry-
landing jetty closely follows the north shore of the bay
of Lakkí, passing the attractive cove of **Kouloúki**, and
reaches **Merikiá** (1.5km from Lakkí), where the pebble
beach, shaded by huge eucalyptus trees, is backed with
empty wharfs and naval building dating from the Italian
Occupation. The valley of hills, both natural and artifi-
cial, inland from here is perforated everywhere with **war-
time tunnels**, galleries and ammunition deposits: one of
these now houses a small **War Museum** (*generally open
daily in summer only 10.30–1; T. 22470 22109 for information*), whose entrance is marked by a compound containing a fighter-jet, armoured car and other vehicles. This is
a collection of memorabilia relating to the Dodecanese
Campaign and the Battle of Leros in 1943. Beyond on the
hill to the left, 200m inland, is an interesting Late Mediaeval church: the western end (?narthex) of the original
structure, cut down into the rock, has partly collapsed.
In the domed crossing, the chapel of **Aghios Zacharías**
has survived. As so often on Leros, the hanging bell here
is a converted war relic. Beyond Merikiá, 400m after the

asphalt ends, the road rounds a corner and ruined Italian military buildings are seen on the hillside opposite. Below in the valley is the double church of **Aghios Spyridon** and Aghia Paraskeví. An ungainly concrete porch of the 1970s hides the fact that this a 14th century building. The north chapel has **paintings** of different periods on both its north and south walls: on the north wall there is a smaller *St George with Dragon* at a lower level (14th century) with the superimposed larger figure painted later; on the south wall, the *Archangel*'s face has been destroyed during the Turkish occupation. The track ends at Katsoúni, a small fish-farming community by the entrance to the bay.

LAKKI TO AGHIOS PETROS

(*West, 3km*)

From beside the hospital building in Lakkí, a road signed to Fytório and Kamaráki leads into rolling panoramic country with good possibilities for walking, and for flowers and birds in the spring. Conspicuous, on a knoll at the centre of these upland hills, is the whitewashed chapel of **Prophítis Elías**. Some patches of mosaic floor and a massive counterweight-stone for an olive press, can be seen in front of the west end; another, similar block is incorporated in the niche to the left of the apse. The track south from here leads to the modern monastery of the Holy Angels (*open for visits 4.30–7.30*), standing above a gorge which drops down to the sea in Goúrna Bay. Behind and above it is the square low-domed church of **Aghios Petros**—a compact, 14th century structure built into the south side of an **Early Christian basilica**, whose foundations can be traced to the north; in the construction of its apse some eroded column stumps are visible. The Early Christian church, in turn, was built over an ancient building—a dressed and drafted corner-stone of which, can still be seen *in situ* below the northwest corner of the existing porch. The white buildings of the Chora and the monastery of St John on Patmos are visible directly across the water to the northwest.

LAKKI TO DRYMONAS

(*Northwest, 5km*)

Less that 500m north from the shore, the land begins to rise: here, amongst gardens and orchards, can be found the older neoclassical houses that predate the Italian occupation. On the road that leads to Goúrna Bay and the airport, after less than 1km and on a curve in the road opposite a splendid four-square balconied mansion, is the fine church of **Aghios Ioannis Theologos** to the right, reputedly built as the result of a visit to Leros by Hosios Christódoulos, the founder of the monastery of the same dedication on Patmos. The design of the church is unusual and striking even from outside, from where it is clear how the central domed space is flanked by two transverse vaulted units to west and east—the latter with an apse which is decorated on the exterior with patterned brick work. (There are similar patterns, high up on the south wall.) This is the original core of the church: it is clear where there has been the addition of later side aisles to north and south. The presence of Early Christian fragments, lying outside as well as incorporated into the construction of the cupola drum, indicates that there was probably a much earlier predecessor on this site. In the interior (currently under restoration and stripped of its plaster), it can be seen how the basic 11th century church was modified by the Knights of Rhodes in the 14th century, to accommodate a Latin liturgy and a different architectural taste, by the addition of the side aisles which help define a western-style nave. The Knights also put in groin-vaults and narrowed the longitudinal focus by introducing a pointed arch in a new wall which filled the space between the original 11th century piers (SW and

NW) supporting the cupola. Patches of **13th century painting** on the walls of the original structure survive in places—one, of notable artistic distinction, shows *St Mary of Egypt receiving Communion*. The church is a good example of how a Byzantine (Orthodox) structure was adapted for a different kind of cult, during the brief period of the rule of Western (Latin) overlords.

The fertile area around Aghios Ioannis Theologos, and up across the saddle towards Goúrna, is marked by many fine and prosperous houses of the 19th century, with well cared-for gardens. Just before the road reaches the **bay of Goúrna**, is the tiny church of the **Panaghia Gourlamáta**, hidden from sight amongst olive trees in a fold in the hill. (*The church is difficult to locate and is best reached from the opposite direction: i.e. climbing back out of Goúrna Bay and Drymónas towards Lakkí, c. 60m after the first sharp bend, a scarcely visible sign points right (west) to the church, through a gap between some houses.*) The simple stone structure of the early 14th century, with the remains of a narthex or subsidiary structure to its west, still preserves some **original wall-paintings**—clearest of all being a compelling *Deësis* (Christ, his Mother and the Baptist) with a running inscription below, carrying the barely legible date, 1324. Below, at the shore of Goúrna Bay, the road continues north past the '*Caserma Regi-*

na'—another relict of Italian occupation, once military quarters, now holiday apartments—towards Kokáli; the sharp left turn leads into **Drymónas** village. At the western extremity of the road along the waterfront is the tiny 14th century church of **Aghios Giorgios** (with traces of wall-paintings) built into the rocks by the water.

LAKKI TO XEROKAMBOS

(*South, 5km*)

The British were the first to begin to organise the sheltered and hidden southeast corner of Lakkí Bay, at **Lépida**, into a naval base; but it was the Italians who developed it most intensively after 1923 and established the 'G. Rossetti Air Base' there, out of which soon grew the need for the creation of the town of Porto Lago. The densely treed area was originally the property of a wealthy Greek from Leros who worked in Cairo, Nikolaos Tsigadas, whose villa and gardens here were expropriated by the Italians and used as an officers' club. In 1923, Florestano di Fausto made designs for the two large buildings visible on the south shore—the long **Air Force Officers' Quarters** and the much more classical Administration Building to its west—which has something of the look of a villa on the

Italian Lakes. All these buildings are now part of the *Leros National Sanatorium* (or Mental Illness Institutions) and are therefore generally out of bounds to visitors.

As the road climbs to the south from Lépida, the site of **Palaiokástro** can be seen on the left, crowning the low ridge between the bays of Lakkí (behind) and of Xerókambos (ahead); it is reached by a steep track from the main road. What is seen immediately—the whitewashed **church of the Panaghia** and the main enclosure wall—is not particularly old: but immediately below the chapel to the east are well preserved stretches of **ancient wall** in the precise, isodomic masonry typical of the 4th century BC, created from large, slightly rusticated blocks which have been drafted at the corners—the whole structure then reinforced by another course internally. The extent of the walls suggests that more than a tower stood here—probably a larger fortress, possessed of excellent controlling views of the two important bays of the south of the island, and with good sight-lines to the ancient acropolis of the city on the summit where the Knights' castle now stands above Aghia Marina. A hastily erected mediaeval fortification, which now lies in rubble below, has also been raised on top of the walls here at some point. Traces of **Early Christian mosaic** in five colours in front of the west door of the chapel show that there was also a Palaeochristian church on this site.

From the quiet fishing harbour and village of **Xerókambos** below (4.5km), are magnificent views of the north of Kalymnos: this *marine landscape can be further enjoyed by taking the early-morning caïque from here to Myrtiés in the bay of Telendos on Kalymnos, and returning with it, if desired, the same afternoon.

Five hundred metres along the eastern side of the inlet, a steep path leads down to the shore where the minuscule chapel of the **Panaghia** '*Kavourádaina*' (Virgin of the 'crab-fisher') is built into a pyramidal cleft in the rocks, in the place where an icon was reputedly found by a crab-gatherer. Inside the chapel is a charming, recent icon of the Virgin in an aureole in the form of a crab.

AGHIA MARINA &
THE NORTH OF THE ISLAND

Aghia Marina (5.5km due north of Lakkí), although the island's second port, is really the heart of the island. With attractive architecture, and a generally more radiant atmosphere and position than Lakkí, it is busy, full of variety and has none of the lassitude which pervades the island's principal port and its flat lagoon. It occupies the position of what must also have been the ancient port, below a natural acropolis, which is now crowned by the impressive castle. Aghia Marina is the port for—and is contiguous with—the island's administrative capital Plátanos on the saddle above, which in turn spreads down the opposite side of the saddle to another attractive, south-facing harbour—Pandéli. To the north, the houses of Aghia Marina line the shore of the bay of Alínda, merging first into Krithóni and then Alínda itself. In this attractive and varied complex of settlements are found the island's museums, squares, water-fountains, principal churches, festivities, finest houses, shops and offices—in short, most of its life. These different, but contiguous, entities are covered below in the order in which they are encountered coming on the main road north from Lakkí.

PANDELI & THE CASTLE

The east coast of the island comes into view from the road, high above **Bromólithos Bay**: contrary to its name, which is redolent of chemistry and translates as 'dirty or smelling rock', this is a clean shingle bay, backed by steep wooded slopes. At its southern end is the cove of **Tourko-pigáda** ('Turkish well')—quieter, steeper, pine-clad and only accessible by foot. These two bays are the southern extension of the village and bay of **Pandéli**, a mass of white, flat-roofed houses which faces south below the castle, from an attractive shore, lined with fish-tavernas. On the ridge to the north are several windmills: six more, immaculately restored, line the road which leads from behind Pandéli up to the castle.

The impressively-sited **castle of Pandéli** (*open Wed, Sat & Sun 8–1, 3–7*), which was substantially repaired after damage incurred during the Second World War, is the principal mediaeval monument on Leros, occupying the island's most panoramic site which was once the acropolis of the ancient settlement of *Leros* from which a few vestigial pieces of masonry have been incorporated into the fortifications. It is a massive complex consisting of three successive enclosures: the inner two, originally of 10th or 11th century Byzantine construction, were later strengthened in the 14th century; the third, much larger, outer enclosure was built in the early 14th century by the Knights of St John. This was the northernmost stronghold of their territory. When Cristoforo Buondelmonti, the Florentine traveller and antiquarian, came to Leros in c. 1417, he observed that the population of the area retired within the castle's walls at night for protection. The Knights' presence here was by no means always welcome; in 1319 their garrison was killed by the islanders, who wished to return under the protection of Byzantium: it was forcibly re-taken by the Knights the same year. Although mentioned in late 11th century deeds of donation from the Emperor in Constantinople to Hosios Christódoulos, the founder of the monastery of St John on Patmos, the castle's structures today are mostly those of the 14th century, and contemporary with Péra Kástro on Kalymnos.

Entrance of the enclosure is by a small gate protected by the massive, projecting southwest bastion. The path leads up to the **church of the Panaghia tou Kastrou**, whose plain design derives from the fact that it was originally an armoury, adapted in the 17th century into a church (by the addition of an apse and a *loggia* on two sides), so as to house a miraculous icon. Some Byzantine fragments of *templon* screen and of an *ambo* are incorporated into its fabric: the interior is dominated by the fine carved icon-ostasis and the unusual pulpit. Attached to the church is a small and well-displayed **Ecclesiastical Museum**, containing liturgical vestments and items, and a number of 18th and 19th century icons of quality.

To the south is the gateway into the **inner fortifications**, leading through a tunnel with finely constructed barrel-vaulting overhead and the original paving under foot; rooms, some vaulted, one of which was formerly used as a chapel, lead off to the side. The passage emerges into a confined space between the two oldest enceintes which constituted what was the entirety of the original Byzantine fortress. A number of modifications were made to this by the Knights, such as the unusual projecting corridor from the northeast corner, added to protect the north side of their new, outer enclosure-walls, and the postern-gate low down in its northeast corner.

PLATANOS

The steps down from the castle lead into the heart of **Plátanos**, the island's capital which is given elegance by its many stately **neoclassical houses**, often finished in unusual and attractive colours. From the town's roof-scape stand out the narrow high-shouldered churches perched on the steep slopes. The finest houses and gardens are in the area of *Od. Asklepíou* which climbs the slope opposite that of the castle: some of these were the island residences built by the rich businessmen of Leros who had emigrated to work in the Greek communities of Cairo and Alexandria after the island reverted to Ottoman rule in 1830 after a brief flirt with independence. To the right, at the beginning of the street is the **church of the Stavrós**, with a fine row of columns in Rhodian marble surmounted by Byzantine capitals, in its south porch. The street is named '*Asklepíou*' because it is believed that the spring towards which it leads on the northeast slopes of Mount Meravigli behind, and known as '***Palaiaskloupi***'—itself a corruption of '*Palaion Asklepieion*'—was the site of an ancient Sanctuary of Asklepios. A small statue of Hygieia, daughter of Asklepios, in the Archaeological Museum was found in this area. The ruins of a large aqueduct carrying water from this spring into the town of Plátanos were demolished in 1887.

The road down from Plátanos to Aghia Marina, passes the **Archaeological Museum** (*open daily 8.30–3, except Mon*) newly accommodated in a former School Building of 1882, originally built by the émigré Leriot community in Egypt. The collection is small, but its explanatory material is particularly clear and helpful in understanding the wider context of the pieces exhibited.

In the courtyard outside, to the left of the entrance, is the **mosaic floor** of the Early Christian Basilica at Parthéni. The single exhibition space of the interior is subdivided chronologically, beginning with one of the museum's strengths— the presentation of prehistoric Leros. The quantity of **obsidian** found near Drymónas in Goúrna Bay and exhibited here, is not only evidence of Neolithic workshops on the island but also of a marine trading communication between Leros and Gialí, near Nisyros, and the much more distant island of Milos. A curiosity also from this period is the 'cheese-pot' type of **Late Neolithic vase**—low, foot-less, and with a row of perforations around the rim—used for cooking or cheese-making. One of the museum's other strengths is its collection of Hellenistic artefacts: fragments of the base of a bowl with feet in the form of applied shells; votive **terracotta masks** with singularly beautiful detail; and, from the year 107 BC, a long, clearly **inscribed *stele***, found in 1886, setting out the honours to be accorded to an alien resident, Aristomachos, for his public services especially in maritime affairs; it was to 'be recorded in stone at the Deme's expense'. A votive inscription of a different kind is preserved amongst a group of **Byzantine floor mosaics** in the collection, which reads, 'Lord, Remember your servant, Eutychias'. There are also fine examples of transparent blue and green Byzantine glass.

AGHIA MARINA

More fine neoclassical mansions with walled gardens may be glimpsed from the road between the museum and the shore at **Aghia Marina**, whose handsome waterfront stretches from the ruined structures of Bourtzi at the eastern end to the **Italian Customs House** (still bearing its ceramic plate, '*Regia Dogana*') and Police Building,

both by Rodolfo Petracco (1934/5), and then on past a
number of colourful waterside houses in more vernacular
style as far as the picturesque, almost submerged, wind-
mill at the bay's western extremity. The town is pleasingly
unpretentious and has a number of good shops selling
local produce and breads. Today the eastern promontory
of **Bourtzi** is marked by the ruins of a mediaeval coastal
fortress, whose series of curiously low wide-arched ap-
ertures overlooking the outer entrance to the bay seem
hard to explain in defensive terms. The slopes above have
been the site of continual settlement on Leros from the
Geometric period through to the Middle Ages, as shown
by the density of pottery finds of all periods in the area.
During maintenance works by the municipality, walls
have also been uncovered going down to the level of Roman mosaic floors. Little is to be seen superficially but
near the small church of **Aghia Barbara**, which is higher
up on the slopes to the southeast and is apparently built
over Ancient and Early Christian remains, there survives
the stepped, semicircular structure of a *synthronon*.

ALINDA

The shoreline between Aghia Marina, **Krithóni** and **Alín-da** is as yet not overly built-up; the beaches are generally shaded and the hinterland is verdant and cultivated. At the beginning of the sweep of Alínda Bay proper (*on the inside of the shoreline road, 50m before the left-turn for the road inland to Parthéni*) is the **British and Commonwealth War Cemetery** with memorials to 183 servicemen—poignantly young—most of whom lost their lives during the Battle of Leros in 1943. The first German landings on the island were to the northeast of here and the bay of Alínda itself saw some of the fiercest conflict. (*A visitors' book and information are stowed in the gatepost.*)

THE BATTLE OF LEROS: NOVEMBER 1943

The Battle of Leros, which strictly speaking lasted just over four days, was the culmination of a long campaign resulting in the loss of the strategically important Dodecanese Islands by Allied Forces to Germany. It is generally considered the last British defeat of the Second World War and the last German victory of any strategic importance. Greece and Crete were lost to the Allies in 1941; but when Italy, who then occupied the Dodecanese, surrendered in September 1943, Churchill saw a crucial opportunity to regain some strategic advantage in the Mediterranean and wanted to move quickly to fill the vacuum left by the Italian surrender, to the benefit of the Allies. The United States was not in agreement and saw such an operation as a lost cause at worst, and at best as a distraction from the main battle-front in Italy. Churchill nevertheless considered the regaining of a hold in the Aegean of such importance that he went ahead without American participation. The Germans moved with comparable celerity and consolidated a hold on Rhodes and its three crucial airfields: on 3 and 4 October they overwhelmed the Allied garrisons on Kos, by which time they had also already begun an unrelenting series of air-strikes against Leros. This began with the sinking in the port of Lakkí on 26 September of two destroyers—the Greek *Vasílissa Olga* and the British HMS *Intrepid*—with considerable loss of life: five days later the Italian destroyer, *Euro*, was also sunk. In addition to fighting at a numerical disadvantage, a decisive factor for the Allies at Leros was that they lacked the air-cover which was fundamental to success. On 12 November a German invasion-fleet landed on the northeast coast of Leros. British forces were too thinly spread and had poor communications within the island. The fighting was intense and the loss of life considerable for four days. On 16 November the British surrendered and 3,200 of their soldiers were taken prisoner. Samos was attacked by German forces the next day, but the island, together with Ikaria, Fourni, and the smaller Northern Dodecanese Islands, was rapidly and successfully evacuated by the Allies. German forces held these islands until their eventual defeat in May 1945. The Battle of Leros formed the basis for the novel (and later film) *The Guns of Navarone* by Alistair MacLean (1957).

There is a small **museum of the Battle of Leros** and the Dodecanese campaign on the upper floor of the **Bellenis Tower** (1925), a turreted mansion in red Egyptian stone, set back amongst trees from the shore-side road at Alinda. This curious building was erected by an émigré Leriot, Parisis Bellenis (1871–1957), who lived and worked in Cairo, and was a notable benefactor of the island. He built the high school of Aghia Marina which still bears his name. The tower also houses a Folklore Museum (the

Manolis Isichos Collection). (*Open May–Sept daily, except Mon 9–12.30, 2.30–6.30.*)

> The exhibits on the ground floor document the history and culture of the island through domestic objects, musical instruments and equipment for printing and publishing. There is much valuable photographic evidence of demolished buildings and monuments on Leros. On the first floor, are relics from the sunken destroyer *Vasílissa Olga*, and plans and memorabilia of the 1943 battle campaign. Photographs of the island's benefactors and heroes, and works by Leriot artists in the collection give a sense of the islanders' wealth and creativity over the last two centuries.

Beyond the tower, the road continues along the north side of the bay to Panaghiés, where a small stone church of the Panaghia above the shore marks the spot of an Early Christian predecessor. This area—the scene of considerable conflict during the Battle of Leros—is now a stretch of tranquil coves with an occasional taverna or café, and pleasant views of Aghia Marina and the castle.

A short distance inland behind Alínda is the **church of the Tesserakonta Martyres** ('Forty Martyrs') (*First road inland from the shore, to the north of the main road signed to Parthéni and the airport*). In the courtyard in front of the door, the remains of a mosaic floor belonging to an Early Christian basilica which stood on this site would suggest that the coast here was considerably inhabited even in Antiquity.

KOKALI AND AGHIOS ISIDOROS

At the junction, 8.5km from Lakkí and 1km west of the shore at Alínda on the principal road to the north of the island, a road leads southwest (left) to the prosperous and fertile village of **Kokáli** (1km) on the north side of Goúrna Bay. From the western end of the village's waterfront a 100m causeway leads out to the picturesque islet and church of **Aghios Isídoros**. Chapels on such sites as these frequently have pagan antecedents, so it is no surprise to find—just below the platform of the chapel, to your left as you climb up—a block of chisel-worked ancient marble lying on the ground. Under the water, below the southeast corner of the chapel, can be seen the blocks and the rectangular plan of the foundations of an ancient building. The next promontory (east) into the bay is also crowned with a small 19th century chapel (of the Tímios Stavrós) with a large stone threshing circle just to its north. It looks onto the sweep of **Goúrna Bay**, which is shallow and protected, and good for swimming.

THE NORTH OF THE ISLAND

The tranquil north coast of the island at **Parthéni Bay** is reached at 12km from Lakkí. The island's earliest human settlement (Late Neolithic, 3500–2800 BC) was uncovered here at Kontarída, beside the central southern creek of the bay in an unprotected and open coastal position.

A civilian airport, a non-functioning dam, a number of gravel-pits, quarries and cement-works, in addition to several military installations, have compromised what would otherwise be a heavenly corner of the Dodecanese. The natural landscape of low hills, deep bays, islands and coastal marshes, was once the setting for the island's principal sanctuary, dedicated to the cult of Artemis or, more correctly, of the '*Parthenos Iokallis*'—a chaste, female divinity, perhaps of local origin, whose cult became assimilated with that of the greater divinity of chastity and hunting. The setting of the temple (whose remains have not been located with certainty) in a marshy estuary by the coast, has affinities with the sanctuary of Artemis *Tauropolos* at Nas on Ikaria.

ARTEMIS AND GUINEA-FOWL

A particularity of the cult of Artemis on Leros was its odd association with the story of the sisters of Meleager. The latter is first heard of in the *Iliad* (IX. 525 et seq.), where his complex story is told by Phoenix to Achilles in the hope of enticing the warrior out of his retreat into his tent. Meleager had killed the ferocious boar of Calydon which had been sent by Artemis in a fit of pique at having been excluded from an important harvest sacrifice. He was later cursed by the goddess, after killing his mother's brothers in an ensuing fight, deliberately fomented by Artemis, over the spoils of the hunt. When his own sisters (referred to collectively as the 'Meleagrids') were, in turn, inconsolable at Meleager's own untimely death, Artemis—more out of irritation than pity—turned them all into guinea-fowl (Ovid, *Metamorph*. VIII, 542–6), immortalising the sounds of their grief in the plaintive bleeping of the bird, which today bears the taxonomic designation, *Numida meleagris*. These beautiful birds probably frequented the sanctuary here filling the air with the sound of their calls, just as peacocks did at the sanctuary of Hera on Samos.

A passing reference in the 2nd century AD 'Tabletalk'
(*Deipnosophistai*) of Athenaeus of Naucratis (XIV,
655 b&c) mentions a (now lost) work, *On Miletus*,
written by Aristotle's pupil, Klytos of Miletus. Klytos
evidently commented on the fact that the priests
took upon themselves the raising of the chicks of
these sacred birds, and that the '… place where they
are kept is marshy'. The edges of the bay here are still
swampy and the name of the sanctuary is preserved
in the modern name, Parthéni. All that is needed is
for the sound of guinea-fowl to break the prevailing
torpor of the atmosphere.

Ancient remains, once erroneously thought to be those
of the temple of Artemis, can be seen in the centre of the
southern side of the bay. Here, on the summit of the ridge
just to the west of the airstrip (*reached by the road west,
before the airport*) is the platform and base of a square
Hellenistic tower (c. 8 x 8m), probably similar in con-
cept to the tower on Lipsi; the position appears chosen
to command both the entrance to the harbour, and the
fertile land around the bay. The blocks are cut and interlocked with the care and precision typical of 4th century
BC masonry. Other smaller, later buildings have left foun-

dations and square cuts in the rocks, to the south. To the north of the tower an **early mediaeval church**, now roofless but still in possession of an apse, has been constructed almost entirely from blocks of the ancient tower. Two hundred metres further north, along the same ridge (*path below, along east side*), is the early 11th century church of Aghios Giorgios. On the south wall of its interior there is a darkened **wall-painting of St George lancing the Dragon**, dating probably from the 15th or 16th centuries; behind the iconostasis stands a carved slab from the marble *templon* of an Early Christian church as well as other more ancient spolia, now heavily whitewashed. The slab probably came from the Palaeochristian basilica found and excavated here in 1980 when construction work on the airstrip began. Its mosaic floor and other carved elements were transferred to the Archaeological Museum. In the same excavations, the ground-floor of a secular building consisting of workshops and storage areas arranged around a pebbled court also came to light near the basilica. These digs have provided evidence of a continued habitation here through Roman times and the Early Christian period, until the abandonment of the settlement in the 7th century. Today **Parthéni** is a tiny community which lives off fish-farming and the large boatyard.

The area is punctuated with relics of the Second World

War—the peaks all round are marked with Italian military watch-towers; the Italian barracks at Parthéni—
which later served as a prison for political detainees of
Greece's Military Junta between 1967 and 1974—are now
used by the Greek military; and the fateful landings on
Leros of 12 November 1943 were coordinated in Palma
Bay, just east of Plefoútis where the offshore islands are
still used today for military target practice. The **bay of
Plefoútis** (1km east of Parthéni), is a beautiful circular
inlet, backed by olive-groves and hills, and marked by
the former Italian military buildings in the pines at the
southeast corner of the bay—harmless and elegiac, now
that their sting has been removed.

The most remarkable monument here is in the tiny
chapel of *__Aghia Kiourá__, on the rise of the isthmus
separating Parthéni and Plefoútis Bays (1km northeast
of Parthéni). The interior of the recent chapel is decorated with images, painted in 1970 by detainees of the
Colonels' Junta, who were exiled to Parthéni. The **murals**
(executed in a polyvinyl paint which is beginning to blis-
ter) are interesting, but understandably variable in quality. There are several hands at work—amongst them one
who specialised in calligraphy, and another in decorative
borders. Perhaps of greatest artistic merit and simplicity
is the *Deposition* along the north wall. These pictures are

now (technically) protected by law, but only after some were painted over by Orthodox religious enthusiasts who resented their style as incongruent with the Orthodox pictorial tradition. The remoteness of the place and the circumstances of its creation are reminiscent of the *Italian Prisoners' Chapel* on the southern tip of Orkney. Both are moving testimonies of faith flourishing in adversity.

PRACTICAL INFORMATION

85 400 **Leros**: area 54sq km; perimeter 82km; resident population 8087; max. altitude 326m. **Port Authorities: Lakkí**, T. 22470 22224, **Aghia Marina**, T. 22470 23256. **Travel and information: Lakki**, Aegean Travel, T. 22470 26000, www.aegeantravel.gr, **Aghia Marina**, Kastis Travel, T. 22470 22140, www. kastis.eu

ACCESS

By air: Leros has a small airport at the north end of the island (12km from Lakkí), to which Olympic Air operates a daily (morning) summer service. There is also a flight three times weekly to Astypalaia, Kos and Rhodes.

By boat: Two main ports are used on the island: the daily services by catamaran (*Dodecanese Express*), and four times weekly by car ferry (*F/B Nisos Kalymnos*) that ply the route between (Rhodes, Kos) Kalymnos and Patmos (Samos) call at Lakki; from the same port there are late-night ferries to and from Piraeus, four times weekly. The faster *Flying Dolphins* on the routes linking the Dodecanese Islands, use the port of Aghia Marina on the east coast of the island: these run daily in summer only. There are also local services to Lipsi and Patmos from Aghia Marina, and from Xerókambos to Myrtiés on Kalymnos. The latter is worth taking simply for the beauty of the scenery along the way.

LODGING

One of the dozen nicest places to stay in all the Greek islands is on Leros, and is to be recommended above all else: the ***Hotel Archontikou Angelou** (*T. 22470 22749 or mobile 6944 908182, www.hotel-angelou-leros.com*) in Alínda is a fine 19th century neoclassical mansion set in its own gardens a little way back from the shore. The rooms are comfortable and beautifully appointed without being over-decorated, the breakfast is excellent, and the setting in every way a delight. Price is moderate: a rental car is advisable. At the southern end of the island, in Xerókambos, the studio-rooms at **Villa Maria** (*T. 22470 27827*) are very simple indeed, but are given life by the burgeoning flowers all around: the lodgings are peaceful, inexpensive and pleasant.

EATING

Some of Leros's best eating places are *mezé* tavernas, serving a wide variety of small dishes to be taken together with an ouzo or wine. The mezedepoleion '**Dimitris**' has the most imaginative selection: it is signposted from a bend on the main Lakkí-Aghia Marina road above the north end of Vromólithos Bay, and is hidden away beside the steps that lead down from the road. It has a terrace with a pleasant view. **To Koulouki**, beside the shore at Koulouki Bay, just to the southwest of Lakkí, similarly serves hot and cold *mezé* on a peaceful terrace. For a shore-side setting of great beauty and for good quality fish, **To Kima**, on the eastern side of Xerókambos Bay is a reliable taverna. Locals, especially on Sundays, like to eat in the bay of Pandéli (south of the castle). There are three fish restaurants here; of these, **Patímenos**, is the most original and thoughtful in the presentation of its dishes, as well as the least expensive. But the liveliest experience and best value is represented by the small café, which produces a remarkable variety of *mezés*—situated in the tiny 'square' just in from the shore at Pandéli, where the one-way system turns sharply back up to Platanos and Aghia Marina.

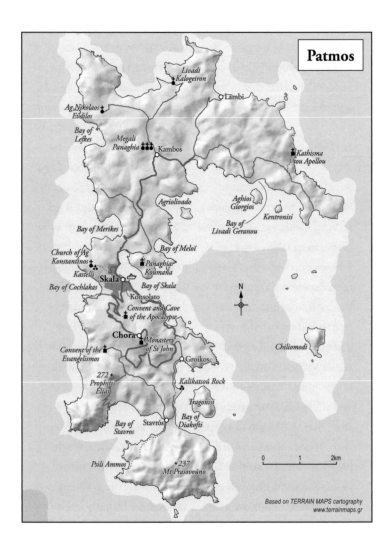

Patmos

Livadi
Kalogeiron

Lambi

Ag. Nikolaos
Evdilos

Bay of
Lefkes

Megali
Panaghia   Kambos   Kathisma
tou Apollou

Agriolivado   Aghios
Giorgios

Bay of   Kentronisi
Livadi Geranou

Bay of Merikes

Bay of Meloï

Church of Ag
Konstantinos   Panaghia
Koumana

Kastelli

Skala

Bay of Cochlakas   Bay of Skala

Konsolato

N

Convent and Cave
of the Apocalypse

Chiliomodi

Chora   Monastery
of St John

Convent of the   Groikos
Evangelismos

272
Prophitis   Kalikatsoú Rock
Elias

Tragonisi

Stavrós   Bay of
Bay of   Diakofti
Stavros

Psili Ammos   237
Mt Prasovoúno

0   1   2km

Based on TERRAIN MAPS cartography
www.terrainmaps.gr

PATMOS

Both in the imagination and in reality, Patmos is so dominated by the great Monastery of St John that it is easy to
forget that there is a lot more to this beautiful island—not
least, its beautiful and architecturally interesting Chora
which, even without the monastery, would be worthy of
attention. The island also possesses a remarkably varied shoreline—deeply indented and modulated at every
point; often backed by dramatic hillsides; sometimes
given character by shoals and banks just below the surface, or marked above water by offshore islets and eroded
rock-stacks, such as the memorable Kalikatsoú Rock; and,
in some places, it is even lined with strands of agate peb-
bles, as at Lámbi. The island is in effect the jagged tip of
a volcanic caldera which extends under water to east and
south, and for this reason its slopes are mostly bare with
outcrops of eroded igneous boulders and its heights are
dramatic and panoramic.

Though chic and well-organised today, the island appeared sufficiently windswept and remote to the Roman
Imperial authorities for them to consider it a suitable
place of banishment for the elderly patriarch of Ephesus,
St John the Divine. Then, almost exactly 1,000 years later,

an energetic and clear-sighted monk came here on his own spiritual exile, fleeing the noise and distraction that disturbed the brotherhood he had created in the mountains of Kos and intent on building a remoter monastery on Patmos in honour of St John. So great was Christó-doulos's desire for peace and spiritual integrity that he insisted on his builders and their families keeping to a separate area in the northern tip of the island, safely away from proximity to the new monastery. 'The loneliness of the island made me leap for joy: I delighted in its tranquillity, rejoiced that it was untrodden. Its remoteness and dreariness were to me a treasure of cheerfulness', he wrote.

But it is the perennial conundrum of great hermits and great monasteries that in time they become focuses of pressing crowds who come to look, either with the eyes of faith or, more recently, the gaze of a blanker sort of tourism. The Monastery of St John is a tiny and intimate space that can ill accommodate the pressing throngs of visitors today, who on occasions push relentlessly through its sanctuary. It is hard to know what the founder would have made of it all. St John himself might be less amazed; with the insight of the vision he received in the cave of the Apocalypse, he had again and again seen images of 'great multitudes which no man could number ... of all nations

… and tongues'. The secret of a sympathetic visit to the monastery is to go, if possible, early in the morning or late in the afternoon, or else on a day when there are no ships in the port: otherwise it is unlikely that it will reveal its true identity. The presence of the monastery has inevitably conditioned many aspects of the island; one of the most rewarding for the visitor, lies in the quality of devotional art that it has attracted, not only in the monastery itself, but in the icons to be found in the many, rural 'Holy Seats', or scattered hermitages, around the island—such as at the Panaghia Koumána, or in the Convent of the Zoödóchos Pígi.

HISTORY

Only scattered evidence of prehistoric (Late Neolithic and Early Bronze Age) settlement has been encountered on Patmos, mostly in the areas of Kastelli, Kalikatsoú and Kambos. In historic times, the island was inhabited by Dorians, and later by Ionian colonists from Miletus. Patmos is briefly mentioned by Thucydides (*Hist*. III. 33.3) (in connection with the Athenian pursuit of the Spartan fleet in 428 BC), by Strabo (*Geog*. X.5.13), and by Pliny (*Nat. Hist*. IV 70), but never with any significant detail. It had limited water and only minor importance in the Ancient Greek world, even though there appears to have been a sizeable city to the east of the acropolis of Kastelli in Hellenistic times, and a temple to Artemis *Patnia* on the summit where the monastery now stands. The island was a small Roman outpost when St John the Divine was exiled here from Ephesus in 95 AD, at the end of the reign of Domitian. By his own testimony, he received the vision of the Revelation, which is now the last book of the New Testament, during his 18 month sojourn on the island.

After the fall of the Roman Empire, the island, ravaged by Saracen incursions, became depopulated, and we hear almost no mention of it until the moment when its history was to change for ever with the arrival in 1088 of the Blessed Christódoulos—a learned and resourceful abbot from Asia Minor who had obtained the blessing and support of the Byzantine Emperor, Alexios I Comnenus, to establish a monastery on the island in honour of St John. Only three years after beginning the enterprise, Seljuk Turkish attacks forced the monks and the founder to flee the island: Christódoulos died in Euboea in 1093, but his followers returned to complete the monastery according to the instructions he had laid down. Under Venetian occupation after 1207, under the protection of Pope Pius II (Aeneas Sylvius Piccolomini) after 1461, and finally under Ottoman dominion after 1523, the monastery's integrity and independence, bestowed on it originally by the Byzantine Emperor, was respected and preserved, sometimes in exchange for appropriate tribute. Refugees arrived on the island from Constantinople in 1453, and from Candia on Crete in 1669, enriching and embellishing the island's cultural and architectural heritage, although the year 1659 saw the Chora plundered by the Venetian admiral, Francesco Morosini. An influential and long-lived Theological School was first established in 1713; and in the course of the 18th and 19th centuries, a growing mercantile class, based on shipping and trade, brought prosperity to the island and developed the port area of Skala. Immanuel Xanthos who was one of the co-founders of the secret Greek Independence Party, or *Philikí Etaireía* ('Friendly Association') in 1814, was from Patmos. Independence came in 1821, only for Turkish control to be re-imposed according to the terms of the London Protocol of 1830. The Italian occupation after 1912 gave rise to the only instance of coercion to change language and liturgy which the monastery faced in its long history. The island joined the Greek State together with the other Dodecanese Islands in 1948. Over the last three decades, Patmos has become increasingly popular with a discriminating and independent tourism, and strict rules govern the construction and restoration of buildings, especially in Chora. The island's biggest challenge, however, now comes from its popularity with cruise-ship tourism, which risks overwhelming the small scale and sacred nature of its most important monuments.

The guide to the island has been divided into two sections:
* *Chora and the south of the island*
* *Skala and the north of the island*

CHORA & THE SOUTH OF THE ISLAND

From afar the startling white, crystalline appearance of the Chora of Patmos, clustered around its fortress monastery, is visible across the water from points on many of the neighbouring islands: this visible link was important in maintaining authority over the area of its influence. From the port of Skala below, its profile dominates the horizon; often early in the morning it is capped with a passing swathe of fog. The winding road up to it from the port is plied by local buses roughly every two hours out of season, and with greater frequency in the summer. The 3km distance can also be climbed in 50 minutes along the old stone-paved *kalderimi*, or mule-track, which leaves from the southern end of Skala. Half way up the climb, by either route, are the buildings of the **Patmiáda School**, immersed in a grove of cypress and fir trees. This is primarily a theological seminary, founded in 1713 by Makarios Kalogieros and still functioning today. Throughout the vicissitudes of Greek history, it has been a constant focus of academic and spiritual instruction, and represents the more evangelical side of the mission of the Monastery of St John. Below it is the **convent of the Apocalypse** (*opening times are the same as for the monastery of St John—see* *below*). A simple entrance, with a modern mosaic lunette above the door, leads into a small complex of churches and cells which have grown up over the last two centuries, around the reputed site of St John's sojourn on Patmos. Steps lead down to the original part of the complex, where a double church has enclosed the mouth of a shallow cave in the hillside. This is an early 17th century construction, which replaced the original 12th century building which was erected here a couple of decades after the building of the monastery of St John. The part which you enter first (straight ahead) is the chapel of **St Anne**—a dedication made probably in honour of Anna Dalassena who was instrumental in getting her son, the Byzantine Emperor Alexios I Comnenus, to grant the lands and privileges for the main Monastery. To the right is the inner portion— the **cave of St John the Divine**—which is believed to be the saint's refuge and the place where he received his vision of the '*Apo-calypse*' ('un-veiling'), which is preserved in the Book of *The Revelation*. Tradition holds that the two silver-framed niches to the right of the iconostasis mark the spot where the elderly saint rested his head, and (to the right of it) put his hand to raise or support himself. The ledge of rock further to the right is supposedly where his amanuensis, Prochoros, rested the parchment on which he wrote down the words which St John dictated to him. The cave may originally have had a spring. Behind the late 16th century iconostasis, which displays the impressive **icon of *St John receiving the Revelation***, by the Cretan artist, Thomas Vathás (1596), are the remains of some **12th century wall-paintings** which had been covered with whitewash until 1973. One fragment, animated by graceful and symbolic gestures, depicts the dictation of the vision by St John to Prochoros; its surface is covered in graffiti, many of which go so far back in time that they constitute in themselves a point of important historical interest.

ST JOHN AND CAVES

John was probably exiled to Patmos from Ephesus in c. 95 AD towards the end of the reign of Domitian, which had been marked by a period of zealous repression of Christianity. He must have been already in his 80s; he appears to have returned afterwards to Ephesus (once the proscriptions of Domitian had been repealed following the Emperor's assassination in September 96 AD), and to have died there around the year 100. It is supposed that he is the same John who was Jesus's 'beloved' disciple, but it is not certain. Patmos was an insignificant island at the time but which had historic links, through the cult of Artemis, with the city of Ephesus. This cave, with its water, may have been an obvious refuge for an exile too old to begin building a roof over his head. It should be recalled that a long tradition going back to Plato and earlier, saw the darkness of caves as the symbol of a state which had not yet been pierced by the light of higher or divine illumination; caves were lairs of ignorance, appropriate places for the having of visions, and hence they were always popular refuges for hermits and anchorites hopeful of illumination. The vision which St John received here was the greatest instance of this in Christian history. His extraordinary testimony was a gift of hope to the 'seven churches of Asia' to whom it was addressed, that their persecution (of which he himself was a victim) was not in vain, that their persecutors (the Roman authorities) would be decisively destroyed, and that all would be turned to good for the chosen faithful.

In iconographic tradition, it should be observed that there is a spiritual hierarchy implied in the images used to depict the Revelation, by which St John is generally seen higher up and outside the entrance of the cave, while his less enlightened servant, Prochoros, sits hunched within, mechanically writing. John's head is turned away towards the hand of an invisible Almighty above, to whom his right hand gestures in awe, while his other hand opens downwards to his humble servant. In this way, he figures as a conduit for divine wisdom, and part of the mystical pattern by which illumination filters down from the Heavens into the darkness of the human soul.

The paved *kalderimi* continues from above the convent of the Apocalypse, reaching the edge of Chora a short distance below the monastery. A steep street climbs up— doubling back on itself, through an area of fine stone houses built mostly by 19th century ship-owners who wished to be in sight of the harbour below—to the entrance of the Monastery at the summit of the hill (190m a.s.l.).

MONASTERY OF ST JOHN THE DIVINE

The monastery of St John (open Mon, Thur, Fri, Sat 8–1.30;
Tues, Wed 8–1.30, 4–6; Sun 8–1, 4–6. N.B these hours may
vary. T. 22470 31223 for information.)

More impregnable and imposing than almost any other
monastery in the islands, the fortified appearance of the
***Monastery of St John the Divine** is eloquent both of
the frightening insecurity of these scattered islands in the
Middle Ages, and of the material and spiritual treasure
that the walls were designed to protect. Though dedicated
to St John the Divine, the monastery possessed no relics
of him, which would have represented its greatest wealth
had they existed. But from the time of its founding it possessed important manuscripts, icons, and documents, to
which were added a library of valuable incunabula, gold
and silver liturgical objects, antiquities and paintings.
From the very moment of its inception, the monastery
was on the frontier of Christianity with Islam, and only
four years after building had begun its founder was forced
to flee from an attack by Seljuk Turks, never to return. It
is in this context that the massive castellation of the religious buildings, begun in 1088 by Hosios Christódoulos
of Latmos, must be seen.

HOSIOS CHRISTODOULOS

Eleventh century autobiographical texts are rare, but Christódoulos has remarkably left us an integral account of his life in the preamble to the *Rule* he laid down for the monastic community he founded on Patmos. He wrote it in 1091, two years before he died; it recounts in the first person, without apparent embellishment, the course of his life, his encounters with the Emperor in Byzantium and his creation of this monastery. It makes fascinating reading *(see 'Further Reading' below)* and reveals a clear-headed and yet passionate man of great spiritual and physical energy—yet with a normality that speaks to us across the centuries. Born near Nicaea c. 1025, Christódoulos (whose secular name was Ioannis, and whose assumed name, Christódoulos, means 'servant of Christ') felt a calling to the monastic life at an early age. He appears to have visited Rome in 1054 and subsequently to have continued to Jerusalem where he withdrew to a monastery in the Palestinian desert. Forced to flee ahead of the advance of Seljuk Turkish incursions, he settled at the monastery of Stylos, near the large monastic community of Mount Latmos to

the east of Miletus, of which he was soon appointed
archimandrite. Once again he was constrained to flee
by Turkish incursions, this time to the island of Kos,
where he built the monastery of the Panaghia Kastri-
aní (at today's Palaio Pyli). He organised a mission to
Mount Latmos to salvage whatever had been left of
the valuables, manuscripts and books after the Turkish attacks. He had what was saved sent to Constantinople; most was retained at Haghia Sophia, but some
of the items were gifted back to Christódoulos by the
Patriarch. In this period he developed relations with
the court of Byzantium, with the Emperor's mother
and with Alexios I Comnenus himself, of whom he
requested official blessing for his project to leave
Kos—because it was too 'noisy' for his ascetic life—
and to settle on Patmos. The Emperor granted him
the whole island as well as lands on neighbouring islands, principally Leros and Lipsi, gave him a boat
and dispensed the monastery from tax obligations
in a signed and sealed *chrysobull* which is exhibited
today in the Treasury. The monastery of St John
was fortified to protect the monastic community as
well as to safeguard the precious manuscripts that

Christódoulos had salvaged. In 1092, almost four years after founding the monastery, he and his fellow monks were forced to flee once more by Turkish attacks. They fled to Euboea where Christódoulos died in March 1093: the possessions—principally books and icons—which he left in his will to the monastery became the heart of its library and treasury. The monks returned with his remains in 1095 to complete the work they had begun under his guidance.

Subsequent history

Already by the time of the Fourth Crusade the monastery had acquired wealth from its land revenues as well as a certain international, or rather pan-Christian, prestige. In the Deed of Partition of 1204, it was largely left free and independent by the Venetian victors; and then, after 1306, the Knights of Rhodes accorded it similar privileges since their presence on Patmos might only have served to attract Turkish reprisals. After Suleiman the Magnificent's defeat of the Knights in 1523, the monastery wisely acknowledged Turkish suzerainty and in return was once again left largely to continue its life undisturbed. In 1713 an important Theological School was founded which continued to benefit from Ottoman tolerance until the Dodecanese passed under Italian occupation in 1912. The Italian authorities tried to impose language and other restrictions on the Monastery, and in 1935 attempted to create an independent Dodecanesian Church which they hoped eventually to subsume into the Catholic Church. The school continued to function with difficulty in hiding. Today the monastery still preserves an independence within the Greek State. It must rank as one of the most successful and long-lived, independent and self-governing monasteries of the Byzantine world.

The site

It appears from ancient spolia (some inscribed), incorporated into the original fabric of the building, as well as other pieces and inscriptions from the surrounding area, that the monastery was built over the remains of a temple dedicated to Artemis *Patnia*. An important inscription (now in the Treasury—*see below*) attests to the legend that Orestes brought the cult of Artemis to Patmos from Scythia and was cured of his post-matricidal madness by the goddess as a result. Another clear, but fragmentary inscription of the early 4th century AD, refers to the founding of a church to St John during 'the ministry of the venerable Bishop Epithymetos'. This may have been the first Christian building to be erected over the pagan temple, and would probably have been in ruins when Christódoulos began constructing the present buildings.

The walls

The enceinte of walls stand to between 16 and 18m in height all round, with only one protected entrance on the north side. These were constructed as an almost windowless, crenellated curtain in the first building campaign of the 11th century, and then substantially strengthened in the 17th century by the addition of the impressive scarps or batters which are the exterior's most visible characteristic today. This is seen best on the north and northeastern sides, where the batters project most massively. The whole complex was extended in the 16th and 17th centuries to the south; in this period the ramp of steps leading up to the north entrance was also added, including the projecting terrace supporting the beautifully proportioned chapel of the Holy Apostles, built in 1603. The (un-scarped) western wing was added, last of all, in the 20th century.

The courtyard

From the machicolated entrance-gate, a steep corridor leads up into the cobbled courtyard which is greater in depth than in width. Additions to the main church have encroached on its already intimate space, which now is like a well of light, unforgettably characterised by the high buttress-arches overhead, with their delicately pointed form. These date from the addition in 1698 of the double-storey arched gal-

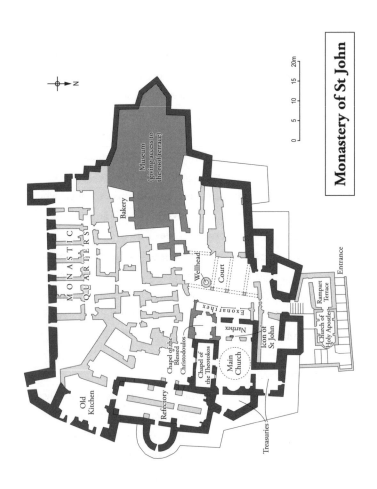

Monastery of St John

N

0   5   10   15   20m

Museum (giving access to the roof terrace)

Bakery

MONASTIC QUARTERS

Wellhead

Court

Exonarthex

Narthex

Icon of St John

Chapel of the Blessed Christodoulos

Chapel of the Theotokos

Main Church

Old Kitchen

Refectory

Treasuries

Church of Holy Apostles

Rampart Terrace

Entrance

lery to the south in dressed ashlar stone, known as the '*Tza-fara*', which is principally a residential wing for the monks. Immediately to the left is the entrance into the original 11th century *catholicon*, preceded by a narthex and **exonarthex**, added in the 12th century. Much of the four-arched colonnade and **balustrade** which define the exonarthex is composed of spolia, both from the temple of Artemis and from the Early Christian church on the site—ancient columns in marble from Fourni (one with spiral fluting), and one balustrade pilaster in the unmistakable **red jasper** from Iasos on the coast of Asia Minor opposite Patmos. The narrative wall-paintings here, which mostly figure scenes and miracles from the *Life of St John*, date from the 19th century. Decorated stone surrounds frame the beautifully carved 17th century **wooden doors**, with an image of the *Annunciation*, giving access to the narthex.

The Narthex and *Catholicon*

Passing from exonarthex to **narthex**, one moves from light into dark, as if into a cave; the narrow space is given further significance by the Monastery's principal *icon of St John the Divine; what we see today is principally a 15th century repainting of great beauty, over an original 12th century icon. The size is impressive (approximately 110 x 75 cm), but it is the finely-modelled robe and, above all, the eyes and brow of great dignity and compassion, which command attention. The Saint holds a book open at the first verses of his Gospel; behind is a small ink-well and pen. The whole is surrounded in a fine original metal frame. The 16th century **wall-paintings** all around have been blackened by candle-smoke and also 're-touched' in the 19th century; but where they are starting to be cleaned (on the south and north faces), rich colours (especially a cinnabar red) are emerging. The small chamber to the south of the narthex is a chapel containing the bones and **relics of Hosios Christódoulos**, brought back from Euboea by his followers after his death and kept in a repoussé silver casket.

The dark and tiny domed space of the *catholicon*, on an inscribed-cross plan, is a refuge from the heat, the light and the winds. There is nothing grand or sophisticated in its cramped and overly tall proportions; this is part of Christódoulos's original building campaign and reflects his simple and ascetic aspirations for the place. Today, the ornate, gilded **iconostasis** of 1820 dominates the space; just above the level of its rail are a number of minutely caved tableau-scenes. Its richness contrasts markedly with the serene **floor** of marble slabs framed in a polychrome inlay of *opus alexandrinum*; once again, it is a plaque of the red jasper from Iasos that occupies the central place. The two **icons** to either side of the central door of the screen were the gift of Catherine the Great of Russia. The **wall-paintings** are early 17th century Cretan work, and include many beautifully executed images: amongst the finest, are the *Pantocrator* in the dome, the *Dormition of the Virgin* (west), and *St John in the cave of the Apocalypse* (north side). Two doors, one in the north wall (surmounted by a clear marble inscription attributing the construction to 'Nikephoros Laodikeias, 1625'), the other hidden from view in the south east corner, lead into two **former treasury-rooms**, which occupy the secure and inaccessible spaces created between the *catholicon* and the fortification walls of the monastery.

The *Parecclesion* (Chapel of the Theotokos)

The doorway in the south wall of the *catholicon* leads into the *parecclesion*, or **Chapel of the Theotókos (Mother of God)**; (at eye-level to the left side of the doorway as you leave the *catholicon*, is a slanting perforation through the wall, whose interior has been polished by the running of a rope which passed through it and once operated an opening mechanism for the door). It was one of Jesus's last commands that St John should take care of his mother and be constantly with her to the end; for this reason her chapel is found here, contiguous with the main church. As a result of severe earthquake damage in 1956, a layer of 18th century paintings in the interior were removed to reveal the late

12th century works beneath. These represent the **original wall decorations**. The *Virgin and Child Enthroned with Archangels* on the east wall is perhaps the finest work here (*ask for light to be switched on for illumination*). It has the rich costumes and vivid solemnity of much earlier Byzantine painting. Above it, on the same wall, the image is reflected formally in the depiction of the **Hospitality of Abraham**—always considered a symbolic prefiguring of the Trinity. The wall is flat because the pre-existing Refectory wall to the east did not give space for the construction of an apse; as one looks at the food prominently laid on the table before the three angels, it should be recalled that on the other side of this wall was the hall where the monks ate. The paintings here have a clarity and spaciousness which is lacking in the later works in the *catholicon* and narthex. On the opposite west wall of the chapel is the damaged but impressive scene of **Christ healing the Bent Woman**. The side walls are decorated mostly with figures of *Saints and Patriarchs of Jerusalem* (beside the south door)—these last, because the chapel and its decoration was probably the gift of Bishop Leontios, who had been abbot here and went on to become patriarch in Jerusalem in 1176. The wooden iconostasis is of the early 17th century.

The whole chapel has its original marble floor and is built over one of the monastery's all-important cisterns. At the foot of the eastern side of the door into the chapel from the *catholicon*, a perforated, upturned Early Christian capital functions as the **lid for the cistern**. A number of other marble spolia are incorporated into the chapel, such as the Early Christian columns in the corners of the north wall, and the **ancient inscription** towards the right-hand end of the second step below the iconostasis, which probably comes from the pre-existing Temple of Artemis.

The Refectory area

On leaving through the south door of the *parecclesion* under a stone canopy, the early **12th century refectory** lies behind the wall running along your left (southeast). Its form is that laid out by the founder, although it was completed after his death—at first with a simple timber roof, then later modified a century later (possibly after a fire) by the substitution of a vaulted and domed stone roof. Running the length of the room's long axis are the two original **stone refectory tables**, with small individual niches below the counter for each monk to store a bowl and knife. The room is now relatively bare, save for a few immured spolia from the pagan temple on this site, but it was originally completely painted. The remains of painting visible today are mostly on the wall by which you enter (west). There are three distinct phases of **paintings** here. The few that remain from the first campaign of c. 1180 (contemporary with the *parecclesion*), are on the flat wall of the blind arch to the north of the door in the west wall: the upper portion of four *Saints* can be seen, while above are sections of two scenes—the *Appearance of Christ to the Disciples on Lake Tiberias*, and the *Multiplication of the Loaves*. Note how these two scenes have been roughly cut in half by the added thickness of wall which has been built out when the roof was changed from timber to a stone-vaulted structure, and how subsequently, in the second campaign of painting, the artists have continued the same scenes above on the new wall surface. This second campaign of a century later (c. 1280) covers the rest of the wall in this northern half of the refectory and is characterised by dramatic, crowded, scenes of stylised and vigorously modelled figures; especially memorable is the scene of **St Peter on Lake Tiberias** failing to stay afloat as he attempts to walk across the water. The third campaign, executed also in the late 13th century, covers the same wall to the south of the doorway and has a quite different style with fewer modelling-lines and greater emphasis on pose and sentiment, as can be seen in the **Crucifixion** and **Passion Scenes** over the door of entry.

Beyond the refectory to the south are the kitchens and bakery, with ovens at one end and, at the other end, a (purportedly original) 11th century **kneading-trough**, carved like a primitive boat from a single piece of wood. From here a small doorway leads to the cells and living quarters of the monks along the monastery's south side.

The Treasury (Museum) and roof terrace

There are a great many ecclesiastical museums in the Greek Islands—a lot of them not particularly special or interesting: this monastery's *museum is in a different category for the range and importance of items it displays, from pagan through to modern times. It consequently should not be missed. The exhibits are laid out clearly in a spacious environment, specially created for them after the earthquake damage of 1956, in a wing added to the west side of the monastery in appropriate materials and style. Manuscripts, icons and liturgical material are mostly to be seen on the lower floor, while ancient artefacts, wall-paintings and larger items are on the upper floor. This account has space only to indicate some of the more unusual items.

(Behind the ticket-desk can be seen the bulk of an 11th century brick baking-oven.) The first section (manuscripts) is dominated by two exhibits: the early *6th century *Codex Purpureus* with letters in gold and silver (which has oxidized) on a purple vellum, which (though only partial) is one of the earliest surviving manuscripts of the Gospel of St Mark; and the magnificent *Imperial Chrysobull of Alexios

I Comnenus, donating title and lands to Christódoulos for the Monastery. It bears the **Emperor's signature** in red cinnabar at the foot and is crowned by a **heading** as ornate as an Ottoman Imperial *tuğra*. Among the other treasures on show from the library are an illuminated, **8th century manuscript of the *Book of Job***, complete with *scholia*, or learned annotations, and some 15th century texts of Aristotle and the Comedies of Aristophanes.

The icons are mostly of Cretan or Constantinopolitan workmanship and are from all periods—rarest of them all, though, is the ***11th century micro-mosaic icon of *St Nicholas*** (possibly brought by Christódoulos from Mount Latmos), set in a 13th century silver frame. Also worthy of note are: the exquisite 12th century icon of *St Theodore Tyron*; the mid-13th century icon of St James, the Brother of Jesus; and two later 16th century icons—an image of *St John* of great compassion (no. 20), and *St John and Prochoros in the cave of the Apocalypse* (no. 25), with a basket of scrolls hanging in the cave behind them. Virtually the last item in this section is a much damaged icon of *Christ on the Way to Calvary*, believed to be an early work by the Cretan, Domenikos Theotokópoulos, known more commonly in the West as 'El Greco'. On this floor are a great many well-conserved liturgical **vestments**, finely embroidered **stoles** and *epigonatia*, and a section of (mostly Venetian) **metalwork**

and jewellery—often in the form of ships—which belonged to the wives of Patmian ship-owners.

The pride of the antiquities on the upper floor is a magnificent late *****5th century head of Dionysos** in Parian marble: the god's beard and hair, held by a head-band delicately tied behind, is executed with particular fineness. There is also a beautifully carved, marble *****Ionic *acroterion*** which formed the corner of an altar—probably the work of a 5th century BC Milesian workshop: a partner to this piece is on show in the Nikephoreion Ecclesiastical Museum on Lispi (*see pp. 158–9*). The long 2nd century AD **inscription from the temple of Artemis** is of particular interest: it refers to Vera, 10th *hydrophoros* (or priestess) of Artemis, 'daughter of the wise physician Glaukias', who 'crossed the perilous Aegean from glorious Argos [in the Peloponnese] where she grew up' to take up her sacred office here on Patmos. It is this inscription which attests to the legend that Orestes, son of Agamemnon, brought the cult of the goddess to Patmos, on his return from Scythian Tauris. The last line of the inscription in large capitals is the one-word salutation '*EΥΤΥΧΟΣ*'—'Good Fortune'.

From the upper floor of the museum a passage onto the roof-terrace emerges in front of the domed, cube of the **chapel of the Holy Cross**, built in 1598—its rough-cut stone and decorated window frames pleasingly set off against the

whitewashed walls all around. The terrace affords matchless
*views over the whole island and surrounding seas.

The Library (not open for regular visits)

The most outstanding items of the monastery's celebrated
library are exhibited in the treasury, mentioned above. The
library is generally closed, but access may be sought for re-
search purposes or academic interest. Its fame and richness
is a reflection of the special value given to books and manuscripts by the monastery's founder. An inventory made by
Abbot Arsenios in 1200 (which copied an earlier catalogue
of 1103) lists already 330 manuscripts—267 on parchment
and 63 on paper; today there are nearer 1,000 manuscripts,
in addition to all the early printed works and documents
relating to the history of the foundation. They give a valuable picture of the spiritual and intellectual interests of the
monastic community, which in addition to religious works
embraced important classical texts by Aristophanes, Plato,
Xenophon and others.

THE ARCHITECTURE OF CHORA

Following the wishes of Christódoulos, little was built
in the area around the monastery walls until the Sack of
Constantinople in 1453, when 'a hundred' refugee fami-

lies from the capital settled here, creating the new neigh-
bourhood of ***Allóteina***, to the west of the monastery. The
arrival *en masse* of these sophisticated urbanites into the
midst of a community of tenant-farmers gave rise to a
flourishing of vernacular architecture which is particular to Patmos. But these were not the only refugees to arrive: in 1669, a further 'fifty' families from Crete sought
refuge on Patmos after the Venetian capture of Candia,
and created the area of ***Kritiká***, this time to the east of
the monastery. Then, in the early 19th century, the successful ship-owners of the island created their own neigh-
bourhood, between the monastery and the eastern area
of ***Aporthianá***, on the steep northern slope of the hill—
the only point from which the harbour and their boats
were clearly visible. At first the **separate mansions** of
the 16th and 17th centuries were large complexes set in
their own plots of land or in walled gardens; then, with
increasing prosperity and population, and an economy
that required artesans and labourers, the spaces between
these mansions were filled with smaller dwellings, until
the whole area became a contiguous urban texture of
tiny streets and houses, in which the original mansions
were only distinguishable by their larger bulk. Two kinds
of stone, both local, were used: a grey granitic rock, and
a softer beige limestone. Characteristic of the whole set-

tlement are the **dressed stone corners** of houses, and
the beautiful **carved window- and door-frames**. These
are set off by the plaster and whitewash applied over the
stone filling of the walls in such a way that the accents of
the architecture—arches, cornices, frames—are clean and
clear, and stand out enhancing the beauty of the townscape. Roofs are flat for the catchment of rainwater, which
is channelled into deep, flask-shaped cisterns cut into the
ground below. A balance between openness, ventilation
and privacy is achieved by the use of a walled court or
avlí; but, in Patmos, this is often repeated on the upper
floor, and in the large mansions such a space becomes
a grand **roofed verandah**, **vaulted with arches** between
two blocks of the house. This may be seen, for example, in
the Simandíris Mansion, which is one of the few open to
the public today. All these buildings, small and great, grew
organically and were added to over time, giving them a
rambling asymmetry and pleasing irregularity of volume. This, in turn, has created the winding irregularity
of the street plan, where streets and alleys vary constantly
in width and often pass through passageways under projections of the houses overhead. In the end this has led
to the formation of few open, public spaces, and Patmos
remains to this day strangely bereft of the traditional central *plateia*.

COUNTERCLOCKWISE THROUGH CHORA
FROM THE TOWN HALL

Just over 150m west of the entrance of the monastery is the *Demarcheion* (town hall) of 1884: the statue on the north side of the open *Plateia Lotza* ('*Loggia*') in front honours the Patmian hero, **Immanuel Xanthos**, one of the earliest Greek independence fighters who in 1814 founded the Greek Independence Party, or *Philikí Etaireía* ('Friendly Association') together with two other Greek businessmen then working in Odessa, Athanasios Tsakalof and Nikolaos Skoufas. Set back, and to the left of the classical façade of the *Demarcheion* with its disconcertingly shallow pediment, is one of the older buildings of Chora—a house whose window frames are carved with Greek crosses, bearing the date 1598 and preserving on the upper floor the sculpted imposts of a former stone balcony. Fifty metres down the street which begins in front of this house (on the right-hand side of the second street to the left) a small ancient inscription has been immured into the wall, just below eye-level: here the street divides and the branch furthest to the right leads to the *Archontikó Simandíris* and to the early 17th century **convent of the *Zoödochos Pigi*** (*open 8–12, 4–7*). The convent, built around two principal courtyards, intimate in size and full

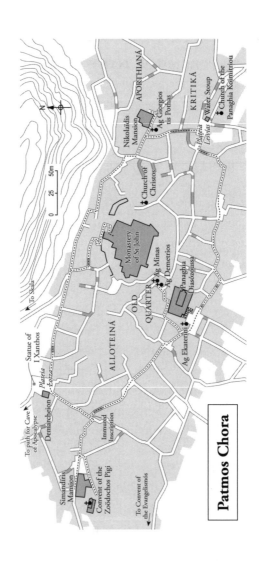

Patmos Chora

of flowering shrubs and climbing plants, is a rich ensemble of icons, wall-paintings and woodwork. Just as in the monastery of St John, there is a main *catholicon*, with a decorated *parecclesion* on the south side: here—since this is a nunnery—the situation is reversed, and the *catholicon* is dedicated to the Virgin Mary, while the *parecclesion* is dedicated to St John. All that is visible here is from the 17th and 18th centuries, but it is complete and of generally high quality—the fine **icon of the *Virgin and Child*** in the narthex with its beautiful carved frame; the simple wooden doors and the (recently cleaned) **cycle of wall-paintings** of the interior, which culminate in a dignified *Presentation of Mary* (right of the iconostasis), and the *Deposition* on the north wall. Only the poorer quality of the faces detracts from the impressive overall effect of rich colour and thoughtful composition.

Almost bordering the convent, and entered from the parallel street one block to its west is the ***Archontikó Simandíris*** (*open 9–1, 5–7*). Built 18 years later than the convent in 1625, the mansion surprises by the airy spaciousness of its interior even though its most attractive feature, the arcaded **upper-floor verandah** with views to the mountain and the sea, has been closed in with glass. The present owner is the eighth generation of her family to live here. The cooler areas below function as work and storage rooms, while the luminous reception and sleeping areas occupy the upper floor. Openness prevails; the building feels more like a community of different habitations than a single residence. The pictures, objects and furniture displayed have mostly curiosity value, but they give a vivid picture of middle-class island life and taste over the last 200 years.

Returning uphill to the junction beside the immured inscription, the street to its east leads around the southern side of the town, with the towering fortifications and scarps of the monastery above and to the left. The large modern **church of the Panaghia 'Diasózoussa'** (the 'Rescuer') is a late 16th century foundation which was entirely rebuilt after the earthquake of 1956: it houses an important Russian icon of the same period. In the area around it are many small stone churches of different ages; although a number of them possess altars made of ancient pagan spolia, their simple vaulted interiors have been whitewashed, and their principal interest is in their carved door-frames and belfries.

After the street has climbed up and turned towards the north into the heart of the *Kritiká* area, it opens out into **Lesvías Square**—one of the few spaces in the town which could be called a main *plateia*, bounded by a couple of tavernas and cafes and marked on its southwest corner by a holy water-stoup, constructed in the form of a small, free-standing stone shrine. The north exit of the square leads under buildings, and follows the curve of the hill around the monastery, towards the north. After 100m, the **Nikolaïdis Mansion** (*open Tues–Sun 11–2*) comes into view down a street to the right. This is a recently restored 18th century residence, quite different in feel and presentation from the Simandíris House: its bare rooms are used to display didactic material on the history and archaeology of Patmos (prepared by the *Department of Antiquities*) as well as some superb examples of **painted furniture**—a pair of cupboard doors, and one of the finest examples of a ***Patmian *ambataros***. The '*ambataros*' is a wooden structure which divides the sleeping area of a room from the main reception area: this is a common feature of Aegean island houses, but on Patmos it acquires a beauty and complexity of its own, combining many functional purposes (storage, privacy, maximisation of space), with ostentatious display in its carved elements and exquisitely painted surface.

THE SOUTH OF THE ISLAND

A kilometre and a half to the southwest of Chora is the **convent of the Evangelismós** (*open daily, 9–11.30*). Built around a 17th century hermitage, the surrounding complex dates from 1937. The principal interest lies in the magnificent **setting** of the convent, dominating the valley to the south, and in the two buildings in its southwest corner—the original hermitage chapel of St Luke, and the church of the *Annunciation*, recently painted with impeccable murals by one of the convent's resident nuns. Immediately to the left on entering, is an exquisite 16th century **icon of the *Annunciation***.

To the south of Chora the landscape is dramatic, declaring its volcanic origin in the scatter of eroded igneous outcrops and boulders at its surface. The island narrows to a thin **isthmus** marked by the church of the Stavrós. Ahead rises the bulk of **Mount Prasóvouno** (237m): to the east is the protected bay of Diakófti, where there is an active boatyard, while to the west, in the bay of Stavrós are salt-pans. The road ends here, but by following the track further south, down the west coast from Stavrós, you climb up and then descend into Patmos's purest sand-beach—**Psilí Ammos**. There is the shade of tamarisk trees, and a taverna which operates in the summer months.

From Stavrós, a route (part track, part road) leads north up the east shore towards Groíkos. The long shallow sweep of the bays of Diakófti and Petra is broken by the conspicuous, eroded form of the **Kalikatsoú** ('cormorant') **Rock**, which is attached to the shore by a flat spit of land and has all the appearance of a Cappadocian outcrop, now that its steep sides and summit have been carved with caves, steps and deep channels for water collection, by generations of worshippers and hermits. No proper study has been made of this remarkable rock; all that can be said is that—as in Cappadocia—its natural hollows have been used by anchorites in the early Middle Ages as inaccessible dwellings, and that the steps and platform cut on and below the summit probably relate to an open-air (?)sanctuary of Aphrodite, which is attested in literary sources. Sherds of clay vessels and stone tools, dating from the early 3rd millennium BC have been found, indicating—as would be expected with such a numinous, natural phenomenon—a very ancient human presence.

The road continues to **Groíkos**, the island's principal resort, set in a sheltered position looking out onto the natural amphitheatre of the bay—the hills grouped around the small island of Tragonísi, with distant views of Leros beyond. Two and a half kilometres further north, the road reaches Skala, through its quiet, southeastern suburb of '**Konsolato**', named after the handful of foreign consulates that opened here in the shipping heyday of the 19th century.

SKALA AND THE NORTH OF THE ISLAND

The activity of **Skala** is a pleasant contrast to the prevailing lifelessness of Chora. Of all the island's many indentations, this bay alone can function as a sufficiently deep and protected harbour. Although the port is ancient, its development as a centre of habitation in recent times dates from around 1600, as does its name, which is taken from a widely-found Italian usage, meaning 'a step' or 'stepping-off point' (i.e. for the main settlement on the hill). It was in this period also that the seas had become sufficiently safe under Ottoman dominion for habitation and stable commerce to begin at sea-level once again, in the place where it had flourished before in Antiquity. Today there are very few ancient remains, but one 19th century traveller noted: 'at the wharf [at Skala] I observed four or five white marble columns, cut and carved in true Greek fashion, and once very likely standing in the portico of some splendid temple to a heathen god, now used as mooring posts' (William E. Geil, *The Isle that is Called Patmos*, 1897). The harbour was taken in hand and improved by the Italians. The 1930 **Customs Building** opposite the main mole, built in the familiar style of Italian colonial design, is a legacy of their occupation. This arcaded architecture stretches inland as far as the animated plateia of the town, with the low, twin-domed **church of Aghios Ioannis** beyond its southeast corner.

KASTELLI

Two hundred and fifty metres north of the main harbour mole, just as the shore-line road curves to the left, the exiguous remains of a Roman construction (now protected by iron railings), to the left of the road, are claimed by local tradition to be the remains of a 'baptismal font used by St John'. The only substantial ancient remains on the island are in fact on the hill-top directly above here to the west at **Kastelli**, where the ruins of a **fortified acropolis** of the 4th century BC still stand. (*The first road turning inland from the south end of the beach, curves round to the left; a flight of steps to the right then brings you to a path, which skirts the east side of the hill, leading up to a saddle with low stone walls and wide views. From here the previously hidden church of Aghios Konstantinos comes*

into view on the top of the rise: the ancient area stretches
south along the ridge from above the church.) The imposing position overlooks three bays: Skala (east), Chochla-
kas (southwest) and Merikas (north). Both along the top
and on the eastern slopes, there are quantities of broken
pottery in the surface of the ground. Analysis of this has
shown continuous occupation from prehistoric times,
through Classical and Hellenistic, and into Roman times.
The surviving parts of the enceinte of walls and towers
are visible on the climb up, the best preserved being the
north and northeast sections, whose compact isodomic
masonry is intact to some height: the **northeast tower**
stands to 3.5m. The stone is volcanic and prone to ero-
sion which has softened the exactly fitting cuts and drafted corners. Just above the church of Aghios Konstantinos
is the northwest tower where a flight of six stairs within
the tower's structure is visible. Given the extent of these
remains, it would appear that Patmos was not as deserted
as is customarily imagined when John was exiled here at
the end of the 1st century AD.

THE NORTH OF THE ISLAND

At the north end of the bay of Skala, a road branches off the principal road to the north of the island and, following the line of the shore, climbs over a rise and drops down to the beach at Meloï Bay. On the rise, a further right branch winds up to the **monastery of the Panaghia Koumána**, founded in 1748 as a 'Seat' of the main monastery of St John. There are many such 'Holy Seats' around the island; they are hermitages, often with a small farmstead attached, which, though physically separate, partake of the community of the main monastery. The church here (1780), built up against the rock, clearly occupies the site of what was once a hermit's cave beside a small artesian well which is still in use. The low domed church has been repainted inside but conserves a particularly beautiful **icon of the *Virgin and Child***, said to be 12th century but which is possibly a little later given its slightly 'Italianising' style. The fine robes and hand of the Infant Christ are beautifully realised, and the eyes of the Virgin, slightly occidental in feel. There are unusual **tiles** on the floor of the narthex, with a stamped and engraved design. Wide views open out from the monastery's burgeoning garden.

The main road north from Skala, passes the attractive, sandy beach of Agriolívado, and leads to the island's only protected and cultivated valley, **Kambos** (4km from Skala), with a scattered settlement, **Ano Kambos**, 600m inland and west of its shoreline resort below. The valley between is dotted with a number of traditional, stone, cuboid houses, in a landscape of igneous boulders and small breaks of vegetation. Beside the attractive *plateia* and modern church of the Evangelismós in Ano Kambos, a road branches left for Aghios Nikolaos, passing (left) the triple **church of the Megali Panaghia**, constituted of three contiguous barrel-vaulted churches, united by an attractive wide porch. The oldest unit—the central church of **Aghia Triada**, with its stone roof, belfry and tiled apse—dates from the 12th century, with the two lateral chapels of the **Panaghia** (S) and **Aghios Athanasios** (N), added a hundred years later, possibly over the site of a pre-existing three-aisled, Early Christian basilica. There are no wall-paintings inside, but there is a fine 16th century **icon of the *Dormition*** in the south church. The even older church of *Aghios Nikolaos Evdilos*—said to be the oldest on the island and built in 1087, one year before the monastery of St John was begun—lies 1.5km further along the road to the west: the simple chapel, heavily buttressed to its north side, has been unfortunately re-painted in recent times. It is to this remote area of the island that Chistódoulos specifically laid down in his *Rule* that the lay-community which had helped him build the monastery should be confined—so that their women and children, their noise, activity and barter, should not be a distraction to the monastic life, as they had been before in his community on Kos.

Leaving by the same road from Kambos, a track to the right after 500m is signed to the monastic **Seat of Livádi Kalogeíron**. The route is panoramic, and the simple rural life of the area through which it passes seems far from the mundanity of Skala. The monastery was founded in 1700 by monks from Mount Athos. A track from here leads east over the ridge to Lámbi (*see below*).

At the north end of Kato Kambos, or Kambos Beach, the road divides: the right branch heads east along the promontory through a wild and beautiful landscape. The bays to the right (south) are particularly quiet and protected; the offshore islands of Aghios Giorgios (with its homonymous white chapel) and Kentrónisi, the wide views of the bay of Skala, and the unusual sandbanks in the water in the **bay of Livádi Geranoú**, combine to make this a coastal landscape of great beauty. Before the final descent to Livádi Yeranoú a track rises to the left, crosses the ridge and descends steeply to the **Kathisma tou Apol-lou**, or '**Apollo's Seat**', an attractively sited monastery, named not after the ancient divinity, but after one of its first hermitic occupants. A spring, a couple of terraces of verdure, a church and a small dwelling complex in a wild and tranquil setting, constitute the hermitage which once again is a 'Seat', dependent on the monastery of St John. On the small promontory below are the remains of a mill and threshing circle; the rock nearby is rich in mineral ores, visible in veins of striking colour.

The island's most famous natural colours, however, are to be found by taking the north branch of the road from Kambos Bay, which leads over the hill to **Lámbi** (6.5km from Skala). This is a long ****pebble shore** facing north and looking towards Samos. At first sight the strand and its small stones seem unremarkable, but closer inspection reveals them to be small fragments of a rock similar to agate, which when wet reveals variegated patterns of ochre yellow shot through with patches of translucent purple, and criss-crossed with striations of white. The mottled effect of the wet surfaces of these stones is of extraordinary beauty.

PRACTICAL INFORMATION

85 500 **Patmos**: area 34sq km; perimeter 72km; resident population 2997; max. altitude 272m. **Port Authorities**: T. 22470 31231. **Travel and information**: Apollon Travel, T. 22470 31324, 31819 ; Astoria Travel, T. 22470 31205, 31975, www.astoriatravel.com

ACCESS

By boat: Patmos has no airport but is well connected by sea to Piraeus, Kos and Rhodes, by *Blue Star Ferries* (twice weekly) and *GA Ferries* (five times weekly); the latter also calls at Kalymnos and Leros en route between Patmos and Rhodes. In the summer season there are daily services by catamaran (*Dodecanese Express*) on the Dodecanese route between Rhodes, Kos, Kalymnos, Leros, Lipsi and Patmos; and four times weekly the car ferry, *F/B Nisos Kalymnos*, runs this same route up from Kos and extends it onwards via Arki and Agathonisi, to Pythagoreion on Samos. *Flying Dolphin* hydrofoils ply the same route daily in summer only, including twice-weekly connections to Ikaria and Fourni. Caïques run local services to the smaller islands, including Maráthi, in high season.

LODGING

Patmos offers a remarkably wide range of hospitality from basic lodgings to overly pretentious hotels: a good halfway house, combining comfort and style is the **Petra Hotel** in Groíkos Bay (*T. 22470 34020, 32567, www. petrahotel-patmos.com*); brand new studio-apartments, overlooking the main bay, can be taken at **Irini Traditional Homes** (*T. 22470 32826, 32556, www.traditional.gr*). For old-fashioned practicality, the **Hotel Skala** (*T. 22470 31343, 31747*), set back in its own garden, is reliable and convenient for ferries, though the breakfast leaves a little to be desired. In the peace and quiet of Old Chora, there are mostly only rooms available;

a couple of the nicest and simplest are those of **Giorgia Triandáfilou** (*T. 22470 31963*) and **Marouso Kouna** (*T. 22470 31026*).

EATING

Chiliomodi, 100m inland of the harbour, to the left of the road to Chora, has excellent seafood and fish, prepared simply and with no frills, in plain taverna atmosphere: the wine is good, and the urchins, small fish and shrimp are the best in Skala. Also in Skala, **Grigoris**, on the waterfront, looks unpromising, but is nonetheless reliable, especially for meat. **Lambi**, on the beach of that name, provides only what is available that day and so can be variable, but the place is quiet and the setting beautiful; **Stefanos**, often just referred to as 'Meloï', with a terrace overlooking Meloï beach, is more consistent and lively and has carefully prepared home cooking.

FURTHER READING

The full text, translated and surprisingly readable, of the *Rule* written by Hosios Christódoulos in 1091 (edited by John Thomas and Angela Constantinides Hero), which contains his 'autobiographical' introduction, can be consulted in *Dumbarton Oaks: Byzantine Monastic Foundation Documents* (published 2000); or at www.doaks.org/typikaPDF/typ033.pdf

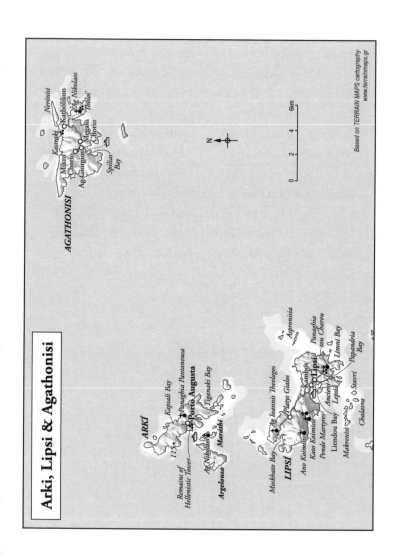

Arki, Lipsi & Agathonisi

Based on TERRAIN MAPS cartography
www.terrainmaps.gr

N

0   2   4   6km

AGATHONISI

Neronisi
Katholikon
Ag. Nikolaos
Kastraki
Tholoi
Mikro Chorio
Megalo Chorio
Ag. Georgios
Spilias Bay

ARKI

Kapsali Bay
Panaghia Pantanassa
Porto Augusta
Tiganaki Bay
115
Remains of Hellenistic Tower
Ag. Nikolaos
Marathi
Argelousa

Aspronisia

Panaghia
tou Charou
Limni Bay
Papendria Bay

Ak. Ioannis Theologos
Platys Gialos
Lipsi
Ancient Lepida
Stavri
Chalavra
Makronisi

Moskato Bay
LIPSI
Ano Koimisis
Kato Koimisis
Pende Martyres
Liendou Bay

LIPSI,
ARKI & MARATHI,
AGATHONISI & PHARMAKONISI

These scattered islands and their countless peripheral islets, framed between Leros, Patmos and the coast of Asia
Minor, and circled on their further horizons by the magnificent mountain profiles of Samos, Ikaria and Kalymnos,
together form a wide seascape of consummate and ever-
changing beauty. This was in Antiquity the Milesian Sea,
and these small and almost waterless islands were too close
to Miletus, the greatest city of this part of Ionia, to have a life
independent of its influence. Traces of ancient settlement
can be seen on them all, but the scarceness of what remains
points to these islands—with the exception of Lipsi—having had only a garrison, a small port-community and a
somewhat seasonal agricultural population. Little more
was possible, because the availability of fresh water was an
absolute and determining factor on how many people such
islands could sustain throughout the year. Evidence of Hellenistic watch towers and forts is common to them all. Current excavations on Agathonisi also point to the primary
importance of their harbours because these islands lived

by protecting and facilitating the immense volume of commercial traffic that passed in and out of Miletus. In essence, they watched one of the principal gateways between Asia Minor and the rest of the Greek world, and their waters were probably busier then than they are today.

Miletus does not exist any more as a city, and a modern political border has separated the islands from the heartland that was their sustenance before. As a consequence they have become remote backwaters whose principal appeal today is that very fact. Their land is poor, with shade and tree-cover at a premium, but their sea is rich both in underwater life and the beauty of its shifting light and landscape. Blessed with limpid waters and a great variety of sand and pebble beaches which are not much frequented outside the high season, these fragments at the very edge of Greece are beginning to attract a quiet and mostly independent tourism. Lipsi and Arki teeter on the edge of losing their tranquility to new building projects. Agathonisi has, better than any, preserved a just balance between the need for tourism and the conserving of a local identity and landscape.

Although walking on these islands is enjoyable and unfailingly affords wide and interesting views, the best way to understand them is by boat. The faithful ferry-boat *Nisos Kalymnos*, which weaves its way up and down this chain, is the simplest solution; there are also many private caïques, based in Patmos and Lipsi, which offer more explorative trips during the summer months. But nothing is better than visiting the islands in a small sailing-craft, in order to reveal their endless variety of shapes, colours and vistas, and to capture some sense of what this corner of the Aegean was like in Antiquity.

HISTORY

Objects and tools of obsidian from Milos found on Lipsi (and now in the island's *Nikephoreion Ecclesiastical Museum*), and similar finds on each one of these islands, bear witness to a Neolithic presence in the entire archipelago. A coincidental similarity between the name 'Lipsi' and that of the nymph who ensnared Odysseus in her grotto, has led some to see Lipsi as Homer's *Ogygia*, home of Calypso. Lipsi is small, with few resources, and it is not surprising that it features little in ancient historical texts: Strabo passes over it in silence; Pliny mentions it cursorily (*Nat. Hist.* V.133). Archaeological remains show, however, that it had a small fortified acropolis, and inscriptions speak of the sanctuary of Apollo *Lepsios* in Hellenistic times—a period in which all these islands were part of the state of Miletus on the Asia Minor coast. Little more than fortifications are visible from Antiquity on the smaller islands, with the exception of the curious vaulted chambers, referred to as *Tholoi*, on both Agathonisi and Pharmakonisi, which probably date from the 5th and 6th centuries AD. Thucydides (I. 116) mentions the waters off *Tragia* (Agathonisi) as the site of the battle between the Samians and the Athenian fleet commanded by Pericles in 440 BC; and Plutarch tells of Julius Caesar's capture by pirates on *Pharmakousa* (Pharmakonisi) in 74 BC (*see box below*).

The subsequent history of the archipelago is obscure until the watershed of 1088, when the Blessed Christódoulos obtained imperial sanction to found the monastery of St John the Divine on Patmos: Lipsi became the monastery's possession from the time of its founding until 1654, after which it has continued to maintain buildings and land on the island to this day. The long-standing link is perhaps responsible for the extraordinary number of churches, hermitages and chapels dotted all over the island. In recent centuries, the islands have followed the history of the Dodecanese, passing under Turkish dominion in 1523, Italian occupation in 1912, playing a commendable part in the Greek War of Independence following the revolution of 1821, and joining the Greek State in 1948.

LIPSI

The well-kept and pleasant *chora* of Lipsi is clustered around a small hill at the back of a wide sweep of harbour comprising two roughly equal bays. The best eating and much of the life of the town take place on the airy **promenade** of the port; while behind it, up a flight of steps, are the narrow streets of the old centre of the village which tend always to lead back towards one of the two tiny protected squares in the area behind the island's principal church. The latter dominates the horizon with its unusually broad form, accentuated by two symmetrical bell-towers. This is the **church of Aghios Ioannis Theologos**, begun in 1931 and built with funds contributed by émigré Lipsiot families in America and Australia. The lavish quantity of liturgical objects and furniture which can be glimpsed behind the iconostasis gives some idea of the generosity of the church's endowment; the interior has particularly fine hanging chandeliers. To the right on entering is kept the miraculous **icon of the *Panaghia tou Charou***—an image comparable to the *Pietà* in western painting tradition, in which the Virgin holds and laments the dead Christ. Inside the glass frame of the icon can be observed some withered lily stalks.

This is the principal relic of the island—a miraculous icon, with an unusual iconography. A lily stalk, dedicated and left at the icon by a grateful suppliant in thanks for a petition granted, was found to revive miraculously from its subsequently desiccated state, and to flower nine days after the Feast of the Assumption on what has now become on Lipsi the Feast of the Panaghia tou Charou (23/24 August). It is said that the miracle repeats each year on the feast, and forms the focus of the island's principal religious celebrations and festivities, involving a procession of the icon across the island.

Behind the church to the northeast is the *Plateia Xanthos*, with a bust of Immanuel Xanthos, the Patmian liberation fighter; the intimate space is animated by a couple of shaded cafés. On the north side of the square is the curious **Nikephoreion Ecclesiastical Museum** (*open weekdays in the summer, mostly between 9.30–1, 4–8; 10–2 at weekends. If closed at these times, ask in the town hall* (Demarcheion) *opposite*). Though chaotically displayed in one small room, this tiny museum should not be underestimated or missed if possible.

The collection is an interesting and mixed *wunderkammer* of artefacts—of which the beautifully carved marble **Ionic corner acroterion of an altar*, produced by a

5th century BC Milesian workshop, is perhaps the prize. (A partner, which comes from the same altar-structure, is exhibited in the monastery's museum on Patmos.) It possesses a timeless formal design, embellished with simple decorative palmettes, and is carved with particularly refined craftsmanship which has the slight imperfection and humanity of true handwork. Amongst the other antiquities on show are: Hellenistic grave objects and *stelai*, *amphorae*, coins (ancient and modern); a large piece from a Byzantine carved *templon*; and dedications found on the island's acropolis, including an **important 2nd century BC inscription** relating to the territory of the island, stating that the decree should be '*set up in the sanctuary of Apollo Lepsios*'. There are relics, stones, dusts and rocks collected or sent from many places: the Holy Land, Asia Minor, Russia, Australia, even the Berlin Wall. Amongst the treasures on paper are two letters (of August 1824) from Admiral Miaoulis, the hero of the Greek War of Independence, and an especially beautiful, 19th century *hand-illustrated book of botany by Dionysios Pyrros. The other natural colours that stay in the memory long after leaving the museum are those of the embroidered *island costumes—reds, mauves and pale pastel greens.

Little remains of the older architectural fabric of Chora, except a few isolated buildings, and one substantial

mansion just behind the post office, facing east. The town
has spread into the areas beyond the original centre in an
open patchwork of houses and gardens, dotted with blue-
domed churches and a quite unexpected Hindu lotus-
stupa (on the hillside to the east of the town)—evidence
of the cultural diversity among the Greeks who have chosen to settle here. Not just the town, but the whole landscape of Lipsi seems punctuated by tiny steeply-domed
chapels in white and blue. These are mostly modern and
tend to have *templon* screens in painted and plastered
masonry: taken singly, they are not particularly notewor-
thy, but they are so numerous and characteristic in form
that together they constitute a unique and determining
element of the island's appearance.

EAST FROM CHORA

The road out of Chora to the south passes below the new
principal ecclesiastical complex on Lipsi, the modern
church of Aghios Nektarios at the lower level, with Aghia
Irini above, and the island's large baptistery to one side.
This road leads to a small headland which is the southern
boundary of the harbour, on the top of which stands the
church of **Aghios Nikolaos**—possibly on the site of the
temple of Apollo *Lepsios*, mentioned in the inscription in

the museum. A finely turned ancient column lies on the ground in front of the church's west end, the gateway is framed with ancient blocks, and a truncated Byzantine column and capital stand against the wall by the west door.

The protected valley further to the south has many fresh-water wells and its sheltered waterfront (now over-grown with reeds) may have been the site of the ancient harbour. To the right of the road, low down in a grove of pomegranates and citrus trees, is the church of the **Pan-aghia Kousélios**. (Locals speak of there being the remains of no fewer than three Early Christian churches below the surface in this narrow valley and that, when digging wells, they almost invariably encounter ancient flagstones.) The church itself has a large ancient block incorporated in its external southwest corner, incised with a Byzantine cross on its west face and a partially legible ancient inscription on its south face, referring to an aspect of the administra-tion of the island and citing a certain 'Apollodoros, son of Herakleitos': there is also a fluted column drum opposite, and a Byzantine capital by the south side. The interior is modern, although the church appears to be built over a much older foundation. The church of Aghia Markélla, a short way inland up the valley, also has ancient spolia in its courtyard (as well as a Second World War shell case which functioned once as its bell).

At the top of the rise, above Aghia Markella, wide views across to Leros open out, and the secluded and sandy beaches of Papandriá and Katsádia appear below. The church of Aghii Panteleimon and Spyridon stands on the hill above, also with a Byzantine capital in front of its entrance. As the road climbs further uphill, a path doubles back to the right after 70m, leading up to the summit of what was the acropolis of **Ancient *Lepsia***. Traces of fortification walls in Hellenistic, isodomic construction are visible, especially at the south east corner of the area, where the base of a tower or bastion can be clearly seen: the later rubble walls nearby have also incorporated large ancient blocks in places. There are good all-round views from the top. A quantity of fallen masonry, some collapsed dwellings and a density of potsherds on the ground, not only on the summit but all down the eastern slope help to give an idea of the extent of the settlement here. The geology of the hill as it descends is interesting too—with calcareous limestone at the top, a stratum of yellow and purple mineral-rich rock below, and an area of very dark limestone at the bottom. From the summit the circular remains of a stone-built **kiln** or furnace can be seen half way down the southeastern slope; then, on the coast below at the east end of the **bay of Limni** (or Limnáki) is another one, better preserved to a much greater height.

These kilns are constructed of rough stone and lined with what appears to be a powdered brick mortar. The deep magenta-red colour of the interior would seem to be the product of ore smelting. The shoreline here is littered with potsherds of all kinds.

A short distance inland from Limni Bay, across a fertile valley, the low—seemingly sculpted—shape of the early 17th century church of the **Panaghia tou Charou** is clearly visible. It is the island's loveliest church, for its broad and graceful form, and it was here that the miracle of the lilies took place. The icon was kept here until it was moved to Aghios Ioannis Theologos in Chora for greater safety. The church's dome is low and the building's overall breadth is enhanced by two side aisles—almost side chapels with their own apses. Just beyond the church's east end are two abandoned farm-buildings, typical of the island's traditional architecture and still in possession of their original design of roof made of wattle, seaweed and compacted mud; inside they both have wine-pressing areas. This is the island's principal wine growing area: further up the road towards Chochlakoúra Bay, on the right just after the asphalt ends, one farmer, Dimitris Makris, sells strong local Lipsi wine from his house.

The road leads on to the beaches of the southeast corner of the island—Xerókambos and Tourkómnima, sep-

arated by a spit of land with the tiny chapel of Aghios
Nikolaos in between. The coast of Turkey is clearly visible
in front. The further bay of Monodendri—with its solitary juniper tree amidst the rocks—can be reached by a
rough path along the coast (30 mins), or more easily by
returning to the asphalt road and turning to the north
and following it until it ends. From here the two striking
islets of **Aspronísia**, just offshore, dominate the seascape:
normally white, as their name implies, of an evening they
catch the light of the setting sun, turning first an apricot-
colour, then pink, then red.

On the return to Chora from Panaghia tou Charou,
just as the road rises, there is a large well-house to the
right-hand side: both the valleys to east and west of the
ancient acropolis hill have fresh water accessible through
wells.

WEST FROM CHORA

From the western end of the harbour of Lipsi, the road
skirts the sandy and pleasant **Liendoú Bay** to the north,
and the area known as '**Kambos**'. This valley (apart from
the hotel and other buildings on its south side) gives
some feel of how Lipsi appeared half a century ago: its
stone-walled fields, scattered trees, partial cultivation and

un-rendered stone houses have altered little since then. At the crest of the hill, the north coast of the island comes into view; almost exactly where the main island road joins from the right, a stony path leads in diametrically the opposite direction up the hill to the left, marked with infrequent red spots. Twenty five minutes of walking brings you to the hermitage church of Stavrós, dwarfed by its apron of stone on the hillside above which collects water into its cistern. On the summit of the hill above is the new **sanctuary of the Five Martyrs**, completed in 2000 at the instigation of the island's energetic priest, commemorating five 'neo-martyrs' who died for their Orthodox faith under the Turkish occupation in the 16th and 17th centuries. The large walled enclosure contains several monuments, two chapels, two sets of lodgings and an aviary with doves and peacocks, laid randomly out over a large barren area, punctuated with concrete flowerbeds. This grandiose monument which fits oddly with the surrounding landscape, has necessitated the construction of a new road which penetrates some way beyond the sanctuary, down to the once isolated **hermitage of Káto Koímisis** on the western shore below. The hermitage, which sits in lush vegetation fed by a slow spring below and looks out over a tiny bay, is a place of rare beauty, but its atmosphere has been eroded by the recent terracing-works and the new road. From the shore, a stone path leads up the western slope of the bay to **Ano Koímisis** (15 mins) where another hermitage, occupied until very recently, sits on a peaceful and panoramic ledge on the hillside above the sea. It consists of a succession of small stone-built spaces—a kitchen, a living room, a narthex or antechapel, and a tiny tri-conch chapel with a cupola. Outside, against the south wall, is a carved and coffered marble fragment from a particular type of Hellenistic grave monument: here the cross-motif in its design has prompted its use in a Christian context. The last hermit to live in these two hermitages, Brother Philippos, left Koimisis in 2000 and died in Lipsi two years later.

A rough track leaves from Ano Koímisis and skirts the contours of the mountain back to the saddle at the Five Martyrs' Monastery (20 mins). From here the new road leads down to the shore and the main island road (20 mins). Turning west, along the road which skirts the shore, the attractive sandy beach of **Platys Gialos** is reached in a leisurely half hour. There are refreshments and a taverna. The final stretch of the road to **Moskháto** can be completed in another 25 minutes. The church to the right of the road, hidden from view of the open sea, is **Aghios Ioannis Theologos**, built over a 17th century predecessor whose foundations can be traced underneath at the east end. The shortest route from Lipsi to Patmos is in fact from this haven at the western end of the island: this may explain the dedication of the church to St John the Theologian. The bay of Moskháto is rocky and narrow; from it, the sun sets over Patmos.

PRACTICAL INFORMATION

850 01 **Lipsi**: area 15sq km; perimeter 39km; resident population 687; max. altitude 277m. **Port Authority**: T. 22470 41133. **Travel and information**: Rena's Travel Agency, T. 22470 41110, renas1022@hotmail.com; **Municipal Tourism Authority**: T. 22470 41185.

ACCESS

By boat: For so small an island, Lipsi is well served from Easter to Oct with frequent connections; out of season, the fast services all stop, and the slower boats are reduced in frequency. From April to Oct the *F/B Nisos Kalymnos*, plies the route from Lipsi (via Patmos) to Arki, Agathonisi and on to Pythagoreion (Samos)—up and down in the same day—four days per week (typically Mon, Wed, Fri and Sun). In the same seasonal period, *Dodecanese Express* catamarans and *Flying Dolphin* hydrofoils between them cover the Kos, Kalymnos, Leros, Lipsi, Patmos route daily. To and from Piraeus there are generally two, occasionally three, connections per week (10hrs) year round.

LODGING

Lipsi's principal 'resort' hotel, open year-round with full facilities, is the **Aphrodite Hotel** (medium price) in Liendou Bay (*T. 22470 41001/2; www. hotel-aphrodite.gr*); there is also the less glossy **Kalypso Hotel**, in the centre of the port promenade, which is functional and has its own restaurant (*T. 22470 41242*). Neither quite captures the simplicity of Lipsi however, and visitors may prefer to stay in one of the many rooms or studios for rent in the town, which represent a good and inexpensive solution. To be recommended because they are both peaceful and set in small, flourishing gardens are: **Studios 'Anna'** (*T. 22470 41126*) and **Kalymnos Studios** (*T. 22470 41102*). They are set back a little way from the centre of Chora; but nowhere is exactly far on Lipsi.

EATING

The best fresh fish and simplest good Greek dishes, without fuss or frills, are to be had at the inconspicuous **Taverna Theologos** on the western half of the harbour promenade; the octopus is prepared particularly well here. But it is generally difficult to eat badly on Lipsi: locals tend to favour the much wider selection of dishes at **Karnagio** (especially at Sunday lunch) which is the last taverna at the east end of the second bay of the port.

Lipsi is famous for its *mávro krasí* ('black wine') which is a dark, sweet, red wine of high alcoholic content, similar to *vin' santo*: it has even been supplied in certain periods to the Vatican as altar wine.

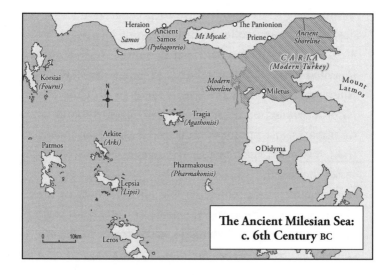

The Ancient Milesian Sea:
c. 6th Century BC

ARKI & MARATHI

The name, 'Arkioí', actually refers to a group of a dozen minuscule islets, called after the largest which was known as *Arkite* in Antiquity, and referred to as *Argiae* in Latin by Pliny. It is an archipelago of rocky, almost tree-less, smooth-shaped islands which together create a seascape of sheltered coves, waterways and turquoise lagoons, thanks to the sand which has settled in several places just offshore. Today the main island of Arkí has four churches, about 50 resident souls, five cows, one horse and a large number of goats. It also has two surprisingly good tavernas, both of which offer furnished rooms for rent. They are situated on the tiny *plateia* at the end of Arkí's deeply indented port which bears the grand Italian name, **Porto Augusta**. The island's life-line is the arrival of the F/B *Nisos Kalymnos*; on occasions, nobody even embarks or disembarks, just a post-packet is tossed ashore, and when the ferry leaves again, a torpor surges back and repossesses the island.

As the ferry boat enters, visible on the crown of the low headland to the west of the new ferry jetty (port side) are the remains of a **Hellenistic watch-tower** of the 4th century BC. (*Once ashore this can be easily reached by a* *short climb up between the quay and the island's emergency heliport.*) Of comparable size with the base of the tower on the acropolis at Lipsi, its remaining lowest courses are constructed in parallel runs of precisely interlocked polygonal blocks—a technique similar to that called 'Lesbian' masonry. The tower here can only have provided protection for the ancient port and surveillance of the channel between Arkí and Maráthi, since it is not sufficiently prominent to have served in a signalling chain. There are traces of retaining walls to the north and of **two lateral walls** that close off an area between the tower and the steep drop at the coast, suggesting that the tower may have been part of a larger complex, modified and reused in Byzantine times as the rubble masonry in the area would suggest.

Some few marble fragments have been found on Arkí (now in the Monastery Museum on Patmos) but little else can be added to our knowledge of the island in Antiquity. Pottery and obsidian from a prehistoric settlement has, however, been found on the hill of Kastro, to the northeast of the harbour. The hill is crowned by the **church of the Panaghia Pantanoússa** today and is reached by a ruined stone-paved mule-track which leads up to the left side of a conspicuous long wall. There are the ruins of some well-built stone houses, with bread ovens still in place; their walls blend mimetically with the barren rocky landscape. From here a path, at first to the northwest, leads eventually down to the northeast shore at the long inlet of Kapsali Bay.

On the east side of the harbour is a break of windswept pines, dotted with eucalyptus and cypress, in which a large house can be glimpsed set back some way above the shore. This is the **Kritikós House**, about which there is a curious reluctance to speak on the island: at the turn of the 20th century most of the islanders were in the employ of Kritikos, who became a collaborator with the Italians during their occupation of the Dodecanese. The house and the mature trees which surround it appear to date from this period, and are at the centre of a walled estate, in which the land has been terraced for cultivation. There are boathouses on both sides of the spit of land on which the house sits. Beyond the nearby church of the Anargyri, a path leads towards the island's most pleasant **beaches**— in particular, **Tiganáki**, at the southeast extremity of the island, where the sand on the floor of the sea creates a turquoise lagoon in an inlet of the rocky coast.

Maráthi

Maráthi (a ten minute crossing from Arkí), immediately appears greener and gentler than its neighbour, its long east-facing bay shaded by tamarisk trees. The island has a population of nine, and two good tavernas on the waterfront, which cater for the excursion visits from Lipsi and have freshly-baked bread and good fish. Both offer the possibility of lodgings: (*Pantélis*, T. 22740 32609, and *Maráthi*, T. 22740 31580). Directly above the shore on the crest of the hill are the remains of a village of stone crofts, deserted in the middle of the last century. On the western hillside, amongst the ruins grouped around the tiny church of **Aghios Nikolaos** are what appear to be the remains of a large **vaulted storage-barn** or cistern dating apparently from the Early Christian era, immaculately lined with brick tiles in patterns. This curious structure, together with the Early Christian fragments and spolia in front of the church, suggest the presence of a small stable community here in the 5th and 6th centuries AD. Another similar construction is to be seen by the shore in the northeast corner of the island, in area referred to as Ellinikó; traces of prehistoric settlement have also been found at Vigla, on the high land at the south end of the island.

PRACTICAL INFORMATION

850 01 **Arkí**: area 6.7sq km; perimeter 25km; resident population 50; max. altitude 115 m. **Port Authority**: (Lipsi), T. 22470 41133.

ACCESS

From April–Oct, F/B *Nisos Kalymnos*, stops at Arkí en route between Lipsi (via Patmos) to Pythagoreion on Samos (via Agathonisi)—up and down in the same day—four days per week (generally Mon, Wed, Fri, and Sun). Maráthi has no scheduled service, but can be reached most easily by day-excursion boats which leave from Lipsi or Patmos during the summer season.

LODGING & EATING

There are currently two possibilities for lodging on Arkí—the rooms rented by the two principal tavernas: **Trypas** (*T. 22470 32230*), and Nikolaos (*T. 22470 32477*). Both serve good fresh fish and octopus; **Nikolaos** has well-presented salads and freshly made fava.

AGATHONISI & PHARMAKONISI

Agathonísi (Ancient *Tragia*) has a more interesting landscape than Arkí: it is higher, deeper and better covered
with vegetation. Its colours are intense—the deeply fer-
rous soil, white rock, and the dark greens of the carob
and arbutus trees against an intense blue sea. Because it
rises quite high from the water, it has commanding views
towards Samos, Mount Mycale and the Meander estuary
in Turkey, and towards the long island of Pharmakonísi.
It also has a population just sufficient to give it a strong
and appealing sense of individuality as an island. The
harbour is of a deep horse-shoe shape, sheltering the neat
and attractive port of Aghios Giorgios and a couple of
very protected coves with shingle beaches to the west of
it—first **Spiliás**, and, slightly further round, **Gaidouráv-
lakos**. From the latter, a rough foot-path up the stream-
bed and then the western side of the ravine will lead to
Mikró Chorió—as its name implies, the smaller of the
two older settlements on the island. This tiny village of
mostly abandoned stone houses occupies a hidden and
relatively fertile saddle between an escarpment of volcanic rock to the north and the peak crowned by the chapel
of Aghios Panteleimon to the south. The few houses still

inhabited, grouped around the *Plateía 25 Martiou* (which commemorates the independence insurgence of March 1821 against Turkish dominion) are well-kept, surrounded by flowers and whitewashed in a stark contrast with the ruins around. Mikró Chorió is more easily reached in a 15-minute walk up the concrete road from the harbour (800m).

The steep ascent from the harbour climbs past the church of Aghios Giorgios, divides briefly to accommodate a venerable carob tree, and gains **Megaló Chorió** at the summit of the ridge. Once again, as at the harbour, a noticeable pride in neatness and orderliness, well-cared for plants and spotless streets, prevails in this tiny community which is the island's capital. Beyond the small *plateía*, at the southeastern end of the village are the joined churches of SS Raphael and John the Theologian. They are new constructions; but visible to the south east on the saddle below, in a stand of eucalyptus trees, is another double church of SS Irini and John the Baptist, where an Early Christian column in the courtyard in front suggests the presence of an earlier place of worship.

The most substantial ancient remains on Agathonisi are to be seen at the island's eastern end, an hour's walk from the village along the panoramic road that follows the plateau and then descends through open *maquis* to

the abandoned village of Kathólikon. There are clear
views across to the Turkish coast at Miletus and Didyma,
and south to the island of Pharmakonisi. All that remains
at **Kathólikon** is a well-maintained church and a fish
farm, floating off-shore in the turquoise lagoon waters
between the bay and the islet of **Nerónisi**. The settlement
is a point of reference for two important explorations
however.

- From Kathólikon itself a track leads back *west* to the
  north coast (which can also be reached from below
  the island's heliport to the east of the village). A spit
  of land, projecting from the north coast, encloses a
  natural harbour and protects it from the north wind:
  here, at **Kastráki**, archaeological digs are currently
  revealing the presence of a sizeable **Hellenistic and
  Roman port installation** and fortified enceinte.

- From the junction just above Kathólikon, a clear
  track continues *south* beside a deep, sheltered inlet
  into the eastern promontory of the island, as far as
  the whitewashed chapel of Aghios Nikolaos clearly
  visible on the hillside. At this point a particularly fertile band of soil crosses the saddle of the promontory from southwest to northeast; on its slopes are

the grand ruins of an early, vaulted structure referred to simply as the *'***Tholoi***'—the 'vaults' or 'domes'—for want of any more specific sense of what these buildings actually are. Three contiguous chambers of considerable size, with another transverse chamber, with their vaults mostly whole and solid, stand in an enclosure made of blind and open stone arches. The stone—which was quarried from a spot still visible below the chapel of Aghios Nikolaos—is bound with mortar and raised, in some stretches, in alternating courses of square and flat stones, reminiscent of Early Byzantine constructional technique. The date and purpose of this complex still remain unresolved, with suggested solutions ranging widely from Late Roman baths to a Venetian manor-house of the 17th century. Baths seem unlikely since there is no evidence of waterproof plaster or hypocaust system; the building technique would also suggest a probable date of around the 5th or 6th centuries AD. Anything later—in the seven centuries of insecurity and piracy that followed the 6th century—would be unlikely given such a vulnerable position. Clearly neither religious nor residential in purpose, it is most likely that this was a complex of granaries and storage chambers—a hypothesis given added support by the fertility of the land around, the proximity to inlets from the sea for loading and transportation, and the presence to this day of stone threshing-floors nearby.

One of the few points of comparison for these strange buildings is provided by some similar structures on the island of **Pharmakonísi**—Ancient *Pharmakousa*—22km southeast of Agathonísi. In the bay of Thóli, the island's principal harbour on the west coast, there are four *tholoi*—once again, contiguous vaulted chambers of similar constructional technique. Here, however, they give directly onto the shore—reinforcing the impression of their use as storage buildings. The island has a number of other remains from Antiquity: the lower courses, with drafted corners, of two **Hellenistic towers** in late 4th century BC construction-technique stand near the hill-top church of Aghios Giorgios, and there are the remains of a Byzantine church, some contemporaneous secular buildings, and traces of mosaic floor in the stretch between Thóli Bay and Paliómantra.

JULIUS CAESAR ON *PHARMAKOUSA*

Although mentioned by Pliny, *Pharmakousa* has made few appearances in world history. Its greatest claim to fame is that the young Julius Caesar was kidnapped by Cilician pirates here in 74 BC. The story is told by Plutarch in his *Parallel Lives* (*Caesar*, I. 2) and is designed to give some sense of the impermeable and ruthless confidence of the man. The pirates were ignorant of whom they had seized, and when they demanded a ransom of 20 talents of Julius Caesar, he laughed at their request and offered them 50. It took 38 days to arrange the ransom, during which time the aspiring politician practised writing speeches and poems, which he tried out on his captors. They were, in his view, an unappreciative audience, and the young Gaius Julius threatened jestingly to hang them all. He was freed on receipt of the ransom, returned to Miletus, commandeered a boat and pursued his former captors until he overtook them. He imprisoned them at Pergamon and had them crucified, just as he had earlier jested.

Pharmakonísi takes its name from medicinal herbs which grow in abundance on the island: today—mostly borage, different kinds of sage, and the common culinary herbs. The early 16th century Ottoman admiral, Piri Reis, whose remarkable map of the waters and coasts of the Mediterranean was found in *Top Kapı* Palace in 1929, visited the island, and noted in particular a 'grove of mastic trees'.

N.B. Because of its sensitive frontier location, the whole island of Pharmakonísi is currently occupied by the Greek Military and is off-limits to civilian visits, except by specific permission of the Ministry of Defence.

PRACTICAL INFORMATION

850 01 **Agathonísi:** area 13sq km; perimeter 35km; resident population 152; max. altitude 208 m. **Port Authority** (Lipsi), T. 22470 41133.

ACCESS

From April to October, F/B *Nisos Kalymnos*, stops at Aga- thonísi en route between Lipsi (via Patmos) to Pythagoreion on Samos—up and down in the same afternoon—four days per week (generally Mon, Wed, Fri and Sun).

LODGING AND EATING

Most lodging is at the harbour: **Maria Kamitsis's Rooms**, with a pleasant shaded terrace, are recommended (*T. 22470 29003, 29004*). In the village of Megalo Chorio, **Studios Angeliki** are an attractive alternative (no tel.). **George's** taverna beside the port is good and reliable for fish and salads; **Limenáki**, a little further in, is simpler with perhaps more local colour.

GLOSSARY OF FOREIGN OR TECHNICAL TERMS

acroterion—an ornamental fixture on the extremity of a building

ambo—the pulpit or lectern of an Early Christian church

Archaic period—the 7th and 6th centuries BC

avlí—a courtyard

chrysobull—an official document issued bearing the Byzantine Emperor's gold seal

ciborium—the (often ornate) canopy which covers the altar in a Byzantine church

cinnabar—a brilliant red pigment; naturally occurring mercuric sulphide

Deësis—a pictorial composition in Byzantine art which became current after the 11th century, in which the figure of Christ is flanked by interceding Saints, most commonly Mary and St John the Baptist

deme—the body politic, and (by extension) the land, of an ancient Greek township

dentils—the cut, rectangular, teeth-like decorations on the underside of a cornice

Dioscouri—Castor & Polydeuces, twin sons of Zeus; saviours and protectors of mariners

entablature—the part of an ancient building above the columns (the architrave, frieze, cornice, etc.)

epigonation—a small, Orthodox liturgical vestment, square in form and highly embroidered

exedra—an architectural protrusion or a free-standing structure of semicircular form

'**free cruciform plan**'—design of a church in which the lateral arms protrude freely from the body of the building (cp. 'inscribed cross plan' below)

Geometric period—the 10th-late 8th centuries BC

'**groin vaults**'—intersecting vaults which spring from opposite corners of a rectangular space

Hellenistic period—era of, and after, the campaigns of Alexander the Great, c. 330–c. 150 BC

homopoliteia—a union or fellowship of (neighbouring) cities or states

Hosios—'blessed'; the title given to a beatified individual in the Greek Orthodox Church

immunitas—(of a Roman dependency) exemption from certain, prescribed fiscal obligations

iconostasis—the high wooden screen (generally holding icons and images) which separates the sanctuary from the main body of an Orthodox church, and which with

time came to substitute the masonry *templon* (*see below*)
of earlier Byzantine churches

in antis—(of columns) set between projecting side-walls
or wings (*antae*) of a building

'**inscribed cross plan**' or '**cross-in-square**'—design of
a church whose exterior is square, but within which the
interior space is articulated in the shape of a cross

insula—a block of buildings, constituting a unified sub-
division of a town-plan

isodomic—(of masonry) constructed in parallel courses
of neatly-cut rectangular blocks

kalderimi—a stone-paved or cobbled pathway or mule-
track

kambos—any fertile area near a settlement used for
food-cultivation

loculi—compartments, or excavated rectangular tombs,
for burial

machicolation—a defensive projection out from a
fortified building, often over the entrance or at a corner,
from which projectiles or hot liquids could be dropped
on assailants

martyrion—a building (mostly circular) which en-
shrines the remains of a holy person, similar to, and
deriving from, the pagan *heroön*

naos—the central interior area of a Byzantine church or

the inside chamber of a pagan temple

narthex—the entrance vestibule of a Byzantine church, often running the width of the building

opus alexandrinum—floor decoration in cut stones, whose intricacy approaches mosaic-work

opus sectile—(more general) floor or wall decoration created from cut and inlaid polychrome stones

parecclesion—a discrete chapel attached and parallel to a larger main church

poros stone—any soft limestone of porous composition used for construction

Proconnesian marble—a white marble, veined with grey, quarried on the island of *Proconnesus* in the Sea of Marmara

pronaos—the front vestibule of a temple, preceding the *naos*

pro-style—(of a building) with an entrance or portico of free-standing columns

scholia—explanatory commentary on a classical text

skaphandro—a sealed diving-suit (a Greek version of the Italian word *scafandro*)

spolia—elements and fragments from ancient buildings re-used in later constructions

stele (*stelai*, pl.)—a carved tablet or grave-stone

stylobate—the platform of a temple supporting its

columns

synthronon—the rising, concentric rings of seats for the clergy in the apse of a church

templon—the stone or masonry screen in a church which closes off the sanctuary

tesserae—the small pieces of coloured stone or glass-paste which compose a mosaic

tetrastyle—(of an ancient building) with a portico of four columns

tholos—a round building covered with a vault or cupola, used often more loosely to refer to any large vaulted structure

triglyph—the element in the frieze of an ancient structure which has two incised vertical grooves and three ridges. It generally alternates with the metopes which are plain or decorated square panels

tuğra—the ornate monogram of the Ottoman Sultan

INDEX

Kalymnos continued

Nigel McGilchrist is an art historian who has lived in the Mediterranean—Italy, Greece and Turkey—for over 30 years, working for a period for the Italian Ministry of Arts and then for six years as Director of the Anglo-Italian Institute in Rome. He has taught at the University of Rome, for the University of Massachusetts, and was for seven years Dean of European Studies for a consortium of American universities. He lectures widely in art and archaeology at museums and institutions in Europe and the United States, and lives near Orvieto.